CONTEMPORARY SOCIAL THEORY

General Editor: ANTHONY GIDDENS

This series aims to create a forum for debate between different theoretical and philosophical traditions in the social sciences. As well as covering broad schools of thought, the series will also concentrate upon the work of particular thinkers whose ideas have had a major impact on social science (these books appear under the sub-series title of 'Theoretical Traditions in the Social Sciences'). The series is not limited to abstract theoretical discussion – it will also include more substantive works on contemporary capitalism, the state, politics and other subject areas.

CONTEMPORARY SOCIAL THEORY

General Editor: ANTHONY GIDDENS

Theoretical Traditions in the Social Sciences

This series introduces the work of major figures in social science to students beyond their immediate specialisms.

Published titles
Barry Barnes, *T. S. Kuhn and Social Science*
Ted Benton, *The Rise and Fall of Structural Marxism*
David Bloor, *Wittgenstein: A Social Theory of Knowledge*
Christopher G. A. Bryant, *Positivism in Social Theory and Research*
Mark Cousins and Athar Hussain, *Michel Foucault*
Bob Jessop, *Nicos Poulantzas: Marxist Theory and Political Strategy*
William Outhwaite, *New Philosophies of Social Science: Realism, Hermeneutics and Critical Theory*
Julian Roberts, *Walter Benjamin*
Rick Roderick, *Habermas and the Foundations of Critical Theory*
James Schmidt, *Maurice Merleau-Ponty: Between Phenomenology and Structuralism*
Dennis Smith, *Barrington Moore: Violence, Morality and Political Change*
Dennis Smith, *The Chicago School: A Literal Critique of Capitalism*
Piotr Sztompka, *Robert K. Merton: An Intellectual Profile*

Forthcoming titles
Ira Cohen, *Structuration Theory*
John Forrester, *Jacques Lacan*
Robin Williams, *Erving Goffman*

New Philosophies of Social Science
Realism, Hermeneutics and Critical Theory

William Outhwaite
Reader in Sociology, University of Sussex

**MACMILLAN
EDUCATION**

First published 1987

Published by
MACMILLAN EDUCATION LTD
Houndmills, Basingstoke, Hampshire RG21 2XS
and London
Companies and representatives
throughout the world

Typeset by Wessex Typesetters
(Division of The Eastern Press Ltd)
Frome, Somerset

Printed in Hong Kong

British Library Cataloguing in Publication Data
Outhwaite, William
New philosophies of social science:
realism, hermeneutics and critical theory
—(Theoretical traditions)
1. Social sciences
I. Title   II. Series
300'.1   H61
ISBN 0–333–36314–0 (hardcover)
ISBN 0–333–36315–9 (paperback)

To my parents

Contents

Acknowledgements

During the excessively long gestation of this book, a number of people have read and commented on parts of the manuscript. I owe a particular debt to Anthony Giddens, the editor of this series, and to Trevor Pateman. I should also like to thank Michèle Barrett, Roy Bhaskar, Gareth Morgan, Gillian Rose, Andrew Sayer and Quentin Skinner. I am also grateful to Cambridge University Press for permission to incorporate, in Chapter 4, some material on Gadamer previously published in Q. Skinner (ed.), *The Return of Grand Theory* (Cambridge: Cambridge University Press, 1985).

W.O.

Introduction

The social sciences in the English-speaking world have been through some dramatic changes in the last twenty years in their understanding of their own nature and methods. I shall call this area the philosophy of social science, though it includes the work, not just of philosophers but of very many sociologists and a smaller number of representatives of the other social science disciplines. In describing realism, hermeneutics and critical theory as 'new' philosophies of social science I do not mean to deny that these three movements have a much longer history. Realist philosophies of science are as old as science itself, though their conscious application to the social sciences dates from the early 1970s. Hermeneutic theory is at least 150 years old, and its application to history and the social sciences is not much more recent, while 'critical theory' was developed in the 1920s. All three however experienced a kind of take-off in the 1970s, moving into the space vacated by the previously dominant conception of social science.

Until this time, it is hardly too much to say that there was no philosophy of social science in the English-speaking world. Rather, there was an empiricist or positivist philosophy of science as a whole, primarily oriented to the physical sciences. This was widely held to constitute the methodological ideal to which the social sciences should aspire. *Ad hoc* modifications of the model were proposed to deal with the alleged greater complexity of social reality, the virtual impossibility of experimentation and the severe limitations on prediction, the problems of ideology and objectivity and so on. Only historians were mostly unable to identify their subject with the orthodox view that to explain an event is to be able to deduce it from a general law.[1]

From this point of view, the three philosophical positions with which this book is concerned were distinctly marginal to the practice

1

of the social sciences. Scientific realism, the claim that the entities postulated by science may really exist, and are not merely convenient fictions, was a somewhat arcane tendency within the philosophy of science; discussion tended to centre around microphysics and the problems of quantum theory. Hermeneutics, the theory of textual interpretation, was known to have begotten Max Weber's concept of *Verstehen*. This had traditionally been wrapped up in a lot of Central European verbiage, but Theodor Abel had shown that all it really involved was the filling out of an explanation by invoking a more or less obvious 'behaviour maxim', e.g. that people tend to light their fires when the weather gets cold.[2] Finally, critical theory was beginning to have some impact, with the publication in 1964 of Marcuse's *One Dimensional Man*, but there was not much sense of its general shape, nor of its implications for the methodology of the social sciences. In methodological terms, as well as in its moral pathos, critical theory seemed irremediably exotic and obscure.

I shall not discuss in any detail the way in which these alternative philosophies and methodologies came into the prominent positions which they occupy in modern social theory. First, the positivist tradition and the critiques which it attracted have already been widely discussed. An earlier book in this series by Christopher Bryant provides an excellent survey,[3] as do Peter Halfpenny's shorter *Positivism and Sociology*[4] and Anthony Giddens's article on 'Positivism and its Critics'.[5] Second, an adequate account of the eclipse of positivism would have to pay close attention to very general changes in the intellectual climate in Western Europe and North America and to the institutional expansion of the social sciences. This produced a generation of academics different in many ways from the previous one. Again, though the full history of these processes has not yet been written, their general outlines are quite well understood.

It should be noted, however, that the rise to prominence of the three traditions discussed in this book went hand in hand with the revival of interest in classical social theory, illustrated by the massive output of secondary works on Marx, Weber, Durkheim, Simmel and others. Furthermore, there was a considerable expansion of qualitative as opposed to quantitative methods of empirical research: participant observation, case studies, unstructured interviews and so forth. On the whole, however, we are dealing with a process which was theory-led, rather than practice-led. In other words, it was not so much that sociologists got involved in qualitative research and subsequently developed a theoretical or philosophical rationale for this practice. Rather, one finds a great outpouring of theoretical and programmatic works, generally produced in isolation from empirical research. This was not just a phenomenon of the division of labour characteristic of a growing scientific discipline; it reflected a widespread feeling among sociologists and some other social scientists that the overall character of social theory required radical re-examination.

A crucial element in this development was of course the revival of Marxism both inside and outside educational institutions. The return to Marx was not just vastly larger in scale than the return to Weber or Durkheim. It was qualitatively different, in that the majority of the writers who engaged in it identified themselves as Marxists, often in opposition to sociology and the other social sciences. In terms of the contrast drawn by Tom Bottomore,[6] it was a matter of 'Marxism against sociology' rather than 'Marxism within sociology'. Yet in institutional terms it was still Marxism *within* sociology, in the sense that this work was largely done by teachers of sociology. For this reason, as well as for reasons to do with the intellectual structure and content of sociology, the opposition between the two tended to become less and less clear-cut. Whereas Marxist economists can still be identified in many Western countries as a distinct sub-species of economist, there is no such clear dividing-line between Marxist and non-Marxist sociologists.

The revival of Marxism, then, like the eclipse of positivism, forms a backdrop to the rise of the three traditions discussed in this book. Its impact on them has of course been very different. Hermeneutics and *Verstehende* sociology have generally developed in opposition to Marxism, except where hermeneutics shades off into critical theory. The latter is of course unintelligible except in terms of its Marxist origins, however far it may have departed from orthodox Marxism. The case of realism is more complicated. A realist philosophy of science does not entail the adoption of any particular variant of social theory. On the other hand, Marx's own largely implicit philosophy of science can best be understood as a form of realism,[7] and his conception of scientific practice has strong affinities with that of modern realists. Furthermore, as a matter of fact, realists concerned with the social sciences have mostly been very sympathetic to Marxist social theory.

The three traditions similarly diverge in their critical response to positivism, and this is the central theme of Chapter 1 of this book. I shall argue that the main initial impact of hermeneutics and critical theory was in stressing the distinctiveness of the social sciences from the sciences of nature. Conversely, the realist critique of positivism claimed that positivism had radically misunderstood the *natural* sciences, and suggested that natural and social science may not, after all, be so radically different in their methods.

In Chapters 2 and 3 I move on to a detailed examination of realism as a philosophy of natural science and in its implications for the practice of social science. The remaining chapters discuss the further development of hermeneutics and critical theory, and the extent to which their essential insights may be incorporated into a realist conception of social science. My basic message is an ecumenical one. Unlike many representatives of hermeneutics and critical theory within the social sciences, I see these movements as compatible, in the last analysis, with a broadly realist understanding of both natural and social science.

1

Philosophies of Social Science: The Old and the New

As I said in the introduction, I do not intend in this book to add to the existing literature on positivist philosophies of science. We need, however, to look at them briefly in order to set the scene for the growth of the hermeneutic, critical and realist alternatives. One of the best recent books on positivism distinguishes no fewer than twelve senses of the term.[1] For present purposes, however, we can get by with three variants.

The first is Comte's original formulation in the early nineteenth century. Positive knowledge, so called to distinguish it from the theological and metaphysical conceptions of the world from which it emerged, yields a methodologically unified and hierarchical conception of science, based on causal laws of phenomena, derived from observation. The progress of knowledge is a process by which the individual sciences, each with its own distinct level of analysis, successfully attain the state of positive, scientific knowledge. 'Sociology' (the term is Comte's invention) is the last to achieve this status and provides the coping-stone for the entire edifice of science and the basis of a positivist morality and politics.

This conception was immensely influential in nineteenth-century thought. In the philosophy of history, for example, H. T. Buckle insisted on the need for a science of history based on the operation of universal laws,[2] such as those determining crime and suicide or relating the frequency of marriage to the price of corn. In a rather different way, Marx and Engels, despite their contempt for Comte himself, shared the aspiration to discover 'natural' laws of human social development. Darwin's account of biological evolution gave a further impetus to this way of thinking (and Engels, of course, drew an explicit parallel with Marx's discovery of the laws of social evolution).

The mid-nineteenth century also saw the beginnings of the hermeneutic critique of positivism – a critique whose basic thrust has remained the same right up to the present. The German philosopher of history J. G. Droysen deplored the spread of 'crass positivism' from France and Britain to Germany and published a hostile review of Buckle's *History of Civilisation in England.* Droysen's *Historik* is one of the first documents of the hermeneutic alternative, stressing the distinction between nature and mind/spirit (*Geist*), and the way in which our 'understanding' of the latter is something radically different from our comprehension of natural phenomena.[3]

The second variant of positivism is to be found in the 1920s, in the logical empiricism of the Vienna Circle. These philosophers preferred to avoid the term positivism, since they considered Comte's philosophy of history to be itself metaphysical. Their own critique of metaphysics was sharpened up in a theory of language, according to which propositions which could not be tested and verified were literally meaningless. The other major way in which they diverged from Comte was in their analysis of the relations between the sciences. For them, the unity of science meant that the laws or, more generally, the language of the 'higher' sciences in Comte's hierarchy could be 'reduced' to that of the lower ones. The propositions of sociology could ultimately be analysed down into those of physics or of material-object language. In this conception, the hermeneutic stress on understanding the meaning of social action was a residue of metaphysical thinking. As Otto Neurath put it, intuitive understanding *might* be of some use to the social scientist, but no more so than a reviving cup of coffee.

This conception of science led, in a modified form, to the third variant of positivism which I shall identify here, and which is the most important for our purposes. It has sometimes been called the 'standard view' in the philosophy of science – a term which indicates its dominant position in the English-speaking world in the 20 or 30 years around the middle of this century. Its main representatives were Rudolf Carnap, Carl Hempel and Ernest Nagel, who emigrated from central Europe to the United States, and Karl Popper, who settled in Britain.

Without going into the details of this position here, I need to bring out one of its central elements, and the one which is of most relevance to the philosophy of social science. This is what I have elsewhere called the law-explanation orthodoxy.[4] The basic theme will, I think, be familiar. It is that all science, including history and the other social sciences, is devoted to the pursuit of explanations, which take the form of general laws, sometimes called covering laws. To explain an event is to relate it to a general law, analysed as a universal generalisation. In a rather hackneyed example, the freezing of my car radiator is explained by the general laws governing the behaviour of water plus the low temperature last night (initial conditions). The roots of this conception of explanation lie in Hume's theory of causation, according to which all we can ever observe is the 'constant conjunction' of events, such as freezing temperatures and burst radiators. This is all we can know, and all we need to know for empirical science to be possible.

The 'standard view' formed the basis of a philosophy of social science which, as I suggested in the Introduction, was not really a philosophy of social science at all. Although it had given up the strong Viennese thesis of the reducibility of all other sciences to physics or to material-object language, physics remained the ideal, and this is as important a fact for present purposes as anything else in the modified logical empiricism which predominated in the English-speaking countries around the middle of this century. Despite the early optimism of Otto Neurath,[5] it proved impossible to beat the social sciences into a shape acceptable to this philosophical view of science.

The consequences of this conception can be found in a wide variety of textbooks in the philosophy of social science. The epistemic privilege awarded to physics shines forth from the merest glance at the chapter headings and examples. Generally the social sciences are kept out of the book until the later chapters, when the feast of models is complete; their own offerings are so mediocre that they would lower the tone of the volume.[6]

What exactly was wrong with the social sciences, on this view? More important than difficulties of experiment or measurement or the problem of ideological influences – though these were also a source of concern – was the problem of laws and explanations in the social sciences. Here one may distinguish between the general appeal of the idea that the social sciences might one day obtain a body of laws comparable to the fundamental principles of physics and chemistry, and the much more precise form which this ideal took in empiricist philosophy of science, in which as we have seen, explanation was identified with deducibility from covering laws. No law, no explanation. One of the earliest statements of this view is in Karl Popper's *Logic of Scientific Discovery*, first published in German in 1934.

> To give a *causal explanation* of an event means to deduce a statement which describes it, using as premises of the deduction one or more *universal laws*, together with certain singular statements, the *initial conditions*.[7]

It is this conception of laws and explanation which is the central target of many realist critiques. For the moment, we need only consider its massive implausibility as an account of explanation in the social sciences. Hempel's classic paper, 'The Function of General Laws in History',[8] attempted to resolve these problems. Hempel's aim was to demonstrate that

> in history no less than in any other branch of empirical inquiry scientific explanation can be achieved *only* by means of suitable general hypotheses, or by theories, which are bodies of systematically related hypotheses.[9]

Hempel suggests as an example

> the statement that the Dust Bowl farmers migrate to California 'because' continual drought and sandstorms render their existence increasingly precarious, and because California seems to them to offer so much better living conditions. This explanation rests on some such universal hypothesis as that populations will tend to migrate to regions which offer better living conditions. But it would obviously be difficult accurately to state this hypothesis in the form of a general law which is reasonably well confirmed by all the relevant evidence available.[10]

Difficult, but also irrelevant. It is one thing to assert the importance of comparative evidence about farmers in a similar situation elsewhere who did or did not choose to migrate; such evidence might, for example, suggest further elements in the explanation such as the fact that mobility is something of a tradition in the US and may therefore be adopted more readily than in other parts of the world. But it is difficult not to feel that Hempel's ideal of a historical explanation, compared to which actual explanations are usually incomplete explanation-sketches, is a metatheorist's fantasy.

Michael Scriven reduced this neatly to absurdity by explicating the following (paraphrased) explanation of Cortes's third expedition to Baja California after the failure of the first two: 'The prospect of gigantic booty, and considerable confidence that by leading the expedition himself the previous causes of failure could be overcome.'[11] In a scientifically 'complete' form, this becomes, for example:

(i) All confident wealth-seeking people undertake any venture which offers wealth.
(ii) The third voyage envisioned by Cortes offered wealth.
(iii) Cortes was confident and wealth-seeking.[12]

Not only is the first premise clearly untrue, but the point of the whole analysis is utterly obscure.

I have dealt with the problem of explanation at some length because it illustrates most starkly the paradoxical character of this philosophy of science and the problems it created. As Mokrzycki has pointed out, not only was logical positivism, at least since the time of Neurath, 'a product of a milieu almost completely lacking in contacts with research practice in the social sciences';[13] it also failed almost entirely to fit that practice. The seriousness with which it was taken by social scientists is probably best explained, as Mokrzycki suggests, by the chronic inferiority complex of the social sciences compared to the sciences of nature:

> sociology, together with related disciplines, such as psychology and political science, is in an exceptional position: it is a discipline in which the very status of being scientific is at stake.[14]

The solace afforded to the social sciences by the 'standard view' in the philosophy of social science may seem to resemble that of the therapist who explains an inferiority complex by telling the patient that he or she *is*, in fact, inferior. But it also offered an image of virtue, consisting in the pursuit of quantitative rather than qualitative data, the eschewal of *Verstehen* except in the most trivialised form, and a long-term goal of the search for the general laws without which explanation was by definition impossible. The law-explanation orthodoxy was most unlikely to be satisfied by the social sciences, but they could always try, and some of them attempted this *Gleichschaltung* more seriously than others: social psychology more than sociology, sociology more than history (which, as we have seen, could hardly begin to conform to the law-explanation orthodoxy).

But there was one area where these harsh prescriptions took a more liberal form: the area of ontology. Questions about the nature of the social or of particular social forms could at least be treated as 'mere' definitional, terminological questions which could be resolved *ad hoc* in a non-binding way. This was the kindly face of the received philosophy of science, and it helped to sweeten the pill. Ontological issues, issues about what exists, were resolved into, on the one hand, the postulates of a theory, whether of subatomic particles or class stratification and, on the other hand, meaningless metaphysics. The logical empiricist programme was originally designed to combat 'metaphysics' at the level of general philosophy, but its attack on philosophical ontology extended into the ontologies of individual sciences.[15]

Logical empiricism, then, as it developed into what has been called the 'standard view' in philosophy of science, confronted the social sciences with a curious mixture of parsimony and generosity. As we shall see, it became more and more generous as it mutated into a conventionalism for which, in Feyerabend's extreme formulation, 'anything goes'. The effects of this metatheory have been well documented in the case of neo-classical economics by Hollis and Nell,[16] and in my book *Concept Formation in Social Science* I attempted to make some points along the same lines.[17] This philosophy was of little positive use to the social sciences, but it did provide a powerful set of defences against possible criticism.

In other words, the standard view offered the attractive possibility that the central problems of social scientific concept formation, the construction of the basic terms picking out the essential features of the social world, could be side-stepped by the use of more or less arbitrary definitional postulates leading to formalised theories. I can best show what I mean by referring to the endemic conflicts both within sociology and on its boundaries with other social sciences, such as economics and psychology, which embraced the standard view and the law-explanation orthodoxy more whole-heartedly. The standard view implied the 'operationalisation' of social scientific concepts, the construction of testable and measurable 'indicators' for alienation, *anomie*, authoritarianism or whatever. But for many sociologists this was not an acceptable way of proceeding. They criticised the simplifications and arbitrary assumptions made in empirical research within sociology and the other social sciences. The orthodox response was to say that this is just what science involves, and that if their critics disliked the assumptions, they should formulate their own or restrict themselves to a more traditional (and, in the orthodox view, impossibly old-fashioned) conception of theory.

Those who were not attracted by the orthodox view, or found it irrelevant to the kind of social science they wanted to do, began in the late 1950s to look more closely at alternative philosophies and methodologies of social science. If the standard view had taken out a patent on the term 'science', perhaps one needed to look for other ways of describing the research practice of history and the other social sciences. What I am calling here the hermeneutic critique has a number of different sources. On the European continent, and especially in Germany, hermeneutic theory proper, the theory of textual interpretation, had fed into the philosophy of history in the work of writers like Droysen, Dilthey, Windelband and Rickert, and thence into the emergent science of sociology, represented by Simmel and Max Weber. (Hermeneutic theory itself was radicalised in the philosophical hermeneutics of H. G. Gadamer, which drew on Heidegger's phenomenological philosophy.) Weber's account of interpretative understanding or *Verstehen* could be incorporated without strain into a broadly positivist theory, as was done by Talcott Parsons and Theodore Abel. Alfred Schutz, however, despite his conciliatory attitude towards systematic theory in, for example, neo-classical economics and Parsonian sociology,[18] was generally understood to be launching a systematic challenge to positivist naturalism – a challenge that was pushed forward less politely by Garfinkel and other ethnomethodologists. These European influences thus combined with the existing tradition of symbolic interactionism, especially the work of Herbert Blumer, which had always been strong in the United States even in the heyday of positivism.

At this point, the Central European tradition upstream and downstream of Max Weber was enriched by themes drawn from linguistic philosophy which, although it also originated in Vienna, had been implanted by Ludwig Wittgenstein in Britain, whence it rapidly spread to the rest of the English-speaking world (and to some extent Scandinavia). Peter Winch refers at times to the German idealist tradition, and to local allies such as the philosopher R. G. Collingwood, but his main attack on 'the idea of a social science' was based on Wittgenstein's concepts of 'language-game' and 'form of life'. To understand a society (whether as a member or an observer), is to learn to think in its concepts, which are also in some sense the real basis of its functioning: 'social relations between men (sic) exist only in and through their ideas'.[19] The regularities in social life should not be understood as causal laws, as in the law-explanation orthodoxy, but as based on people following *rules*. Winch was deliberately bringing out the implications of Wittgenstein's work for traditional grand problems in the philosophy of social science. In a more modest mode, the linguistic analysis of John Austin and others was incorporated in various ways into ethnomethodological work on language.

By the mid-1960s, then, it was possible for Karl-Otto Apel to point to the convergence of analytic philosophy of language and the Continental tradition of the human sciences or *Geisteswissenschaften*. For Apel, the tension in analytic philosophy was between its philosophy of science and its critique of metaphysics on the one hand, and its orientation to the *language* of science on the other:

> From this one might conclude: although Analytical Philosophy as a philosophy of science accepts as the goal of science only the 'objectivistic' explanation of facts, nevertheless, the problems involved in the very idea of 'language analysis' must lead Analytical Philosophy 'through the back door' into the midst of those problems which the theory of 'understanding' of the Geisteswissenschaft was designed to cope with.[20]

These connections were made most dramatically in Winch's book, but they can also be found in a wide range of works in the philosophy of action, centred around the theme that human beings are not only propelled by causal influences, but also act for reasons, which are not causes and must be understood in terms of rule-following or some other mode of analysis radically distinct from the identification of law-like regularities.

The upshot of these internal developments within analytic philosophy was that the minority of anti-positivists in the social sciences had a new source of philosophical support to rely upon. If it took them some time to draw these consequences, this was no doubt because the 'linguistic turn' in analytic philosophy had itself taken place without manifestos or other programmatic accompaniments. The public image of analytic philosophy continued for a long time to be that of a modified logical empiricism. Moreover, the literature emerging out of the analytic tradition mostly failed to engage directly with the practice of the social sciences. The analysis of action was often extremely individualistic in focus. Where, as in the work of Peter Winch, due attention *was* given to the social character of action, this occurred within a somewhat imperialistic conception of the primacy of philosophy in relation to the social sciences – a conception which emphasised language to the virtual exclusion of the other dimensions of social life, and thus tended towards a rather static account of society.[21]

The second major anti-positivist influence of this period, that of Frankfurt School critical theory, also took a long time to develop, but this time for more banal reasons to do with differences in language and cultural tradition. By the late 1960s, however, Jürgen Habermas was beginning to attract some attention in the UK and US, and his main work of metatheory, *Knowledge and Human Interests*, appeared in English in 1971.[22] It was another five years before the publication of *The Positivist Dispute in German Sociology*, though Giddens's collection, *Positivism and Sociology* (1974), discussed the debate of 1961 and reprinted papers by Albert and Habermas.[23]

Habermas's critique of positivism in *Knowledge and Human Interests* consisted, in essence, in a general thesis and a special one. The general thesis was that positivism had transformed epistemology, the theory of knowledge, into a mere methodology of science. In his historical discussion of positivism, Habermas attempted to recover the dimensions of philosophical reflection which positivism had obscured: the way in which science was grounded in the fundamental interests in knowledge which set the conditions for possible knowledge of nature and society. In other words, he was restating Kant's transcendental inquiry into the conditions of knowledge, but in the form of a *social* theory of knowledge. The knowledge-guiding interests arose out of the basic interests of human beings rather than the pure functioning of an abstract human consciousness.

This general thesis was difficult to grasp for readers trained in analytic philosophy. Habermas's special thesis, by contrast, could be understood with much less difficulty. This was the triadic model of cognitive interests, in which the empirical-analytic sciences were based on an interest in prediction and control of objectified phenomena, historical-interpretative sciences were oriented towards understanding, and critical social science combined the two in an investigation of the causal obstacles to understanding, based on an interest in emancipation. The special thesis therefore fed into the critique of positivistic social science, where this was seen as a vehicle of technocratic manipulation of human beings and a servant of the status quo in advanced capitalist societies – this being one of the major themes of the revolutionary student movement.

I shall discuss these issues in more detail in later chapters. For the moment, it is enough to note that both the 'hermeneutic' and the 'critical theory' critiques of positivism had extremely little to say about its status as a philosophy of *natural* science. Both Habermas and, by implication, Gadamer, claimed that it was inadequate in the sense that it was *merely* a methodology of science, requiring completion by transcendental (Habermas) or hermeneutic (Gadamer) reflection. But Habermas seemed to have no quarrel with positivism as a methodology of natural science: indeed his characterisation of natural science in terms of a 'technical' interest in prediction and control was a piece of classic positivism, even if it was then turned to anti-positivist conclusions. Habermas was not so much concerned to refute the positivist account of natural scientific methodology, as to limit its intrusion into the realm of social theory. The cost of doing so, however, was to support, somewhat against his will, the methodological dualism, the separation of natural from social science, which had inspired the hermeneutic critique. Like some of Winch's critics, he did not want such a closed border between understanding and causal explanation, but he could link them only, in a rather unconvincing way, in his conception of emancipatory science based on Freudian psychoanalysis and the Marxist critique of ideology. By the mid-1970s then, there were at least two broad traditions of anti-positivist thinking in the philosophy of social science. The problem was that their reference point in the philosophy of natural science was increasingly not just a straw positivism but one which was decomposing into silage.

For while social scientists continued to see a somewhat liberalised logical empiricism as *the* philosophy of science, differing only over whether or not it was applicable to the social sciences, the logical empiricist consensus had turned into something very different. There are differing accounts of what were the crucial steps in this evolution, but the most important is what has been called the 'holistic turn', in which it was recognised that scientific statements cannot be tested in isolation, in a direct confrontation with experience. They get their meaning from the complex networks of metaphors, models and theories in which they are located. Arguments of this kind, anticipated by Pierre Duhem before the heyday of logical empiricism, were turned against it by W. V. O. Quine, Mary Hesse, Rom Harré and others. This holistic analysis of the internal structure of scientific theories came together with a holistic analysis of scientific change, which was presented by T. S. Kuhn as a succession of discrete paradigms or 'disciplinary matrices'. Kuhn's interest was in the history rather than the philosophy of science, but he flirted with conventionalist language, claiming that Lavoisier, after his discovery of oxygen, 'worked in a different world',[24] and the analogies which he drew between paradigm changes and Gestalt switches, religious conversions, etc., had a fundamental effect on the way in which philosophers of science came to think about theory-change. Paul Feyerabend drew the most radical consequences with his polemics 'against method' and his 'anarchistic' or 'dadaist' slogan that 'anything goes'.

Seen from the standpoint of the social sciences, all this looked rather familiar. The more reflective social scientists knew that they held their theories for reasons which were difficult to justify and were probably ideological. Even those who knew they were right had noticed that it was intolerably difficult to convince their opponents. Perhaps this was, after all, not a function of the immaturity of the social sciences but simply *la condition humaine*. The response varied in the different traditions of sociology and the other social sciences. The more relativistically inclined social constructionists in sociology, social anthropology and on the margins of social psychology, were perfectly happy, as were those who had embraced Gadamer, Heidegger or the pre-Socratics. The empiricists, still strong within sociology and stronger still in economics and political science, generally decided to go on playing the game by the old rules. The greatest unease seemed to be felt by those influenced by Marxism. Kuhn's *Structure of Scientific Revolutions* had an initial appeal in revolutionary circles in the late 1960s, not just because of its title but because it gave weight to the idea of a sharp split between radical and bourgeois paradigms or problematics; Marxism could thus brush aside the tiresome quibbles raised by empiricists. At the same time, there was the more important consequence that much conventional work in the social sciences drew its legitimation from empiricist philosophies of science and was therefore weakened by their demise. But Marxists have never felt comfortable with relativism, and in the end it was the apparently relativistic consequences of the new philosophy and history of science which seemed more important and threatening. (For whatever reason, many of the most significant recent contributions to realist philosophy of social science have been made by writers sympathetic to Marxism.)

The holistic turn was much more than a source of sceptical doubts about science (or about the account of science given by empiricist philosophers). In its more positive aspect, it was part of a long overdue *rapprochement* between the philosophy of science and the history and sociology of science. Although some philosophers of science, such as Carnap and Popper, had made substantive contributions to physics, most had avoided examining too closely the practice of science. The philosopher's contribution was seen as being distinct from that of the scientist; its distinctiveness was marked out by slogans such as 'logical analysis', 'rational reconstruction' or the distinction between 'context of discovery' and 'context of justification'.

This arms-length approach was of course parallelled in analytic philosophy of action or in Alasdair MacIntyre's 'conceptual analysis' (*sic*) of the Unconscious.[25] In the philosophy of science, perhaps its clearest expression was in Popper's response to Kuhn. Popper accepted the existence of what Kuhn called 'normal science', science practised within a framework of unquestioned assumptions, but saw it as 'a phenomenon which I dislike (because I regard it as a danger to science)'.[26] Taking up Kuhn's distinction between 'logic of discovery' and 'psychology of research', Popper concluded that

> to me the idea of turning for enlightenment concerning the aims of science, and its possible progress, to sociology or to psychology (or, as Pearce Williams recommends, to the history of science) is surprising and disappointing.[27]

Here, as elsewhere, however, Popper's position found less and less support among philosophers of science. The majority view came to be that, whatever Kuhn's philosophical inconsistencies, he had pointed to important features of the practice of science which required philosophical investigation.

The historically based holism converged with a more holistic approach to the internal analysis of scientific theories – a process set under way, it must be said, by Popper himself in his original critique of Viennese empiricism. Linguistic philosophers and historically sensitive philosophers of science launched a common attack on the distinction between observational and theoretical terms and the ideal of deductive formalisation of theories. Mary Hesse was one of the leading exponents of an alternative conception based on the notions of network and model.[28] On this view, deductivist conceptions misrepresented the structure of scientific theories, making them out to be more tightly integrated both internally and with respect to empirical evidence than they actually were, and also misrecognised their function, as models of natural processes. A closer analysis of the language of science brought out the importance of the notions of model and metaphor. Rom Harré pushed these ideas further into a full-blown realist conception of scientific theory and, in particular, the analysis of causality. Natural necessity was rehabilitated in the analysis of causal relations in terms of the powers and tendencies of things.[29]

The history of these developments, their interconnections and their relation to earlier forms of realism is a complex story which would require a book to itself. For our purposes, it is enough to note tht the search for foundations of knowledge was a kind of self-destruct mechanism at the heart of empiricist philosophy. Logical empiricism had started from two postulates: experience as the foundation of knowledge, and a conception of theory as the interpretation of a logical or mathematical system. The marriage of these two was an unhappy one, marked by frequent separations and reconciliations, with periodic attempts to redefine the 'correspondence rules' linking theoretical statements with observational reports.

The realist solution was to reformulate the problem: to draw the consequences from the conventionalist critique of immediate experience, and to shift the emphasis back from epistemology, the theory of knowledge, to ontology. Given that we have scientific theories, and that on the whole they seem to work remarkably well as an explanation of the world, what must the world be like in order for science to be possible?

2

The Realist Alternative

It may seem paradoxical that a philosophy of science, especially one which calls itself realist, should start from the premiss that science, like humanity itself, is a historical accident. But can this premiss be seriously questioned, except on some creationist view? The paradox is on the other foot, that of the apparently robust epistemologies which allow us to be certain about our experiences but not about that of which they are experiences (the external world, other minds, or even our own bodies). No serious account of knowledge can begin without the assumption that 'to be' is more than 'to be perceived'. And no theory of science is conceivable without the assumption that what we are pleased to call laws of nature operated in the same way as they do now before humans evolved and *a fortiori* before they began to do science. It is, when one thinks about it, an odd philosophy of science which ignores such considerations.

Realism is, then, a common-sense ontology, in the sense that it takes seriously the existence of the things, structures and mechanisms revealed by the sciences at different levels of reality. There is no distinction of principle to be drawn between such assertions and claims about discrete observable 'facts'; the task of science is precisely to explain 'facts' in terms of more fundamental structures, and in the process it may reveal some of these 'facts', such as the observable motion of the sun across the sky, to be, in part, illusions. Not that the sciences are always right in their assertions: substances like phlogiston and the ether may have to be purged from our ontology; atoms may reveal themselves to be not a-tomic at all, but complexly structured entities, and so on. The realist assumption is merely that the existence of such entities is not to be construed as a heuristic assumption, but as a truth-functional

19

assertion like any other, even though we may not yet, and never finally, know whether it is true or false.

The other side of this non-atomistic ontology is a non-empiricist epistemology: one which allows for the complex and often paradoxical reconceptualisations introduced by science. Again, the realist point is that these interpretations *are* hypotheses, in the sense that they are potentially corrigible by further discoveries. In the terms introduced by Roy Bhaskar's *A Realist Theory of Science*, they are the transitive objects of science, created by human beings to represent the intransitive objects of science, the entities and structures of reality.[1] As Bhaskar puts it at the end of his book:

> Things exist and act independently of our descriptions, but we can only know them under particular descriptions. . . . Science . . . is the systematic attempt to express in thought the structures and ways of acting of things that exist and act independently of thought.[2]

Like other philosophical positions, realism can only be understood in terms of its oppositions to other philosophies or, as they are sometimes called, metatheories of science. In this chapter, therefore, I shall begin by contrasting realism with empiricism and with a variety of positions generally termed conventionalist, instrumentalist or pragmatist, which in the twentieth-century context have themselves to be understood as the product of the dissolution of empiricism. In other words, we are not concerned with a timeless dialogue between abstract alternative positions, but with a dynamic process, taking place in real time, in which the abandonment of the simple certainties of empiricism leaves the philosophy of science on a slippery slope towards a position where all claims to truth have apparently to be abandoned and where the choice between alternative theories appears to be a matter of taste or an arbitrary leap of faith. There are basically two possible escape routes from this slippery slope. One is the position generally called rationalist or transcendentalist; the other is the realist position which I am arguing for here. In the second half of this chapter, therefore, the focus shifts to the contrast between realism and rationalism.

Let us begin by looking once again at the contrast between a realist and an empiricist analysis of causal relations. The classical empiricist approach starts from the observation of constant conjunctions between events. J. S. Mill provides a clear formulation of this Humean conception:

> We have no knowledge of anything but phaenomena; and our knowledge of phaenomena is relative not absolute. We know not the essence, nor the real mode of production, of any fact, but only its relations to other facts in the way of succession or similitude. These relations are constant; that is, always the same in the same circumstances. The constant resemblances which link phaenomena together, and the constant sequences which unite them as antecedent and consequent, are termed their laws. The laws of phaenomena are all we know respecting them. Their essential nature, and their ultimate causes, either efficient or final, are unknown and inscrutable to us.[3]

Thus, for example, we observe that water freezes when its temperature falls to 0 °C, and we formulate a law that whenever the latter happens, so does the former. When people ask us why their ponds or car radiators have frozen, we explain that it is because of a fall in temperature. In the other direction, this law enables us to make predictions: we can warn people that if the temperature falls much below 0 °C, their radiators will freeze unless they add anti-freeze. Given that the regularity has existed in the past, we can be confident (*pace* the 'problem' of induction) that it will occur in the future; the law sustains both explanation and prediction.

But even an inquisitive child will feel that there is something unsatisfactory about explaining 'why' something has happened by saying that it always does. If I ask why my train is late, I may be partially reassured to be told that the 8.55 is always late, but even British Rail would hardly dare to offer this statement as an *explanation*. The survival of what came to be called 'covering-law' conceptions of explanation is one of the great puzzles in the history of philosophy; it can only be explained by a pathological fear of ontology and, in particular, of notions of natural necessity.

Realists, by contrast, analyse causality in terms of the natures of things and their interactions, their causal powers (and liabilities). The guiding metaphors here are those of structures and mechanisms in reality, rather than phenomena and events. In Bhaskar's terminology, to start from the experience of constant conjunctions is to conflate three separate domains:

1. the real (made up of entities, mechanisms etc);
2. the actual (made up of events);
3. the empirical (made up of experiences).

But these domains are distinct, and the moves from (1) to (2) and from (2) to (3) are contingent. Events can occur without being experienced and, more importantly, causal mechanisms can neutralise one another in such a way that no event takes place; there is no potentially observable change in reality. The objects on my writing-table are all subject to gravitational attraction, but they are prevented from falling to the ground by the resistance offered by the table. The open window is buffeted by the wind, but is held in place by a metal bar. The healthy state of my body is the outcome of a continual violent combat within it. The hot-water boiler battles away against the effects of the second law of thermodynamics. Unlike a constant conjunction analysis, which logically presupposes that the system within which 'causal' relations are observed is isolated from extraneous influences, a realist analysis of causality can account for the interaction of various causal tendencies within the complex and open systems among which we live, and which we ourselves are.

The latter point is important, for it is a particular virtue of a realist analysis that it enables us to see the parallels between our own causal powers and liabilities and those of other physical objects. Like the higher animals, we can choose to initiate certain causal sequences made possible by our causal powers. Unlike them, we can reflect on those powers and formulate long-term projects to develop and use them e.g. by 'body-building', learning to drive, undergoing psychoanalysis, or whatever. Our reasons for acting, whether we analyse them as causes or as something different, clearly play a part in generating our behaviour. When someone gives up smoking, for example, the outcome is a complex product of physical dependence, habit etc. on the one side, and the reasons for giving up on the other.

The preceding outline of realism has taken the form of a contrast with empiricism, and it is now time to develop this a little more fully. We also need to introduce a further cluster of positions, generally called instrumentalist, conventionalist or pragmatist, which I shall argue need to be understood as a product of empiricism, at least as far as the history of the last few decades is concerned. One of the major problems in the philosophy of science is the lack of agreement in the use of these terms and others, but the basic story is a very simple one. As we saw in the previous chapter, empiricism, whether in its classical Humean form or in the logical empiricism of the Vienna Circle and its followers, is sceptical about philosophical claims about reality. It seeks a bedrock in the analysis of observations (classical empiricism) or observation-*statements* (logical empiricism). For logical empiricism, all other propositions either express logical or mathematical truths or are impossible to verify and therefore meaningless. The statement 'God exists' (or, for that matter, 'God does not exist') is meaningless because no observational evidence has any bearing on the matter. And the same goes for the opposition between 'electrons exist' and 'electrons do not really exist but are merely convenient fictions which we postulate in order to make statements about our observations'. Realism and instrumentalism, the positions represented by the above statements about electrons, are technically 'meaningless' and merely represent alternative languages which, like English and French, are equally available to philosophers. Rudolf Carnap, for example, reported that he 'gradually' came to 'recognise clearly that my way of thinking was neutral with respect to the traditional controversies, e.g. realism versus idealism, nominalism versus Platonism (realism of universals), materialism versus spiritualism, and so on'.[4]

Scientific theories, on this view, are reducible to observation-statements (or more complex constructs built out of observation-statements) and logical-mathematical relations. The problem was that this 'eliminative' approach to theory, as Peter Halfpenny describes it,[5] could not provide an adequate analysis of scientific statements, most of which could not be explicitly defined in observational terms. Observation-statements, for their part, seemed to be theory-laden in all interesting cases, so that the distinction between observational and theoretical terms, in which the latter were more and more 'partially' interpreted by correspondence rules, seemed increasingly difficult to sustain.

In liberalising the connection between theories and experience, empiricism mutated into conventionalism and pragmatism; the original scepticism about theory generated an equal scepticism about experiential data. The sceptical snake had swallowed its own tail; the bedrock had vaporised and it was 'theory all the way down'. In Quine's classic formulation, 'our statements about the external world face the tribunal of sense experience not individually but only as a corporate body . . . The unit of empirical significance is the whole of science.'[6]

Quine himself has retained a modest form of pragmatic realism. In response to the suggestion, made by the realist philosopher J. J. C. Smart, that he had shifted from an instrumentalist to a realist position, Quine emphasised the continuity of his views, taking back in the process what Smart saw as concessions to realism with the assertion that 'existence in its final estate is theoretical'. He went on to repeat this passage from *Word and Object*:

To call a posit a posit is not to patronise it . . . Everything to which we concede existence is a posit from the standpoint of a description of the theory-building process and simultaneously real from the standpoint of the theory that is being built. Nor let us look down on the standpoint of the theory as make-believe, for we can never do better than occupy the standpoint of some theory or other, the best we can muster at the time.[7]

This is the essence of the pragmatist position: truth, reality, existence only have meaning within a theory. Our theories (*contra* empiricism) are underdetermined by observational evidence; in other words the same evidence is compatible with a variety of theories, between which we must choose. The pragmatist, like the empiricist, can use realist language in scare quotes, but considers realist claims, taken straight, to be meaningless, since they go beyond experience (empiricism) or our available theories (pragmatism). We cannot know anything beyond our experience and/or what we are told by 'the best theory we can muster at the time'.

The empiricist aim was to maintain continuity with the sciences, and at the same time to preserve a special position for philosophy as the privileged judge of knowledge-claims. Pragmatic philosophies aim to maintain continuity with science in a rather different way, by giving up the special position of philosophy. In Quine's words: 'The key consideration is rejection of the ideal of a first philosophy, somehow prior to science.'[8] This response followed the gradual abandonment, within the empiricist tradition, of the search for guaranteed foundations of knowledge. As Richard Rorty puts it, the theory of knowledge which emerged as a central philosophical preoccupation with Locke

> is supposed to explain *how knowledge is possible*, and to do that in some *a priori* way which both goes beyond common sense and yet avoids any need to mess about with neurons, or rats, or questionnaires.[9]

Such a conception would not easily avoid giving epistemic privilege to introspection: just as, for Woody Allen, solitary masturbation meant having sex with the person you love most, so for epistemology, our knowledge of our own minds and the impressions which our minds receive are our most precious and reliable epistemic resource. Where the impressions come from, by contrast, is already a somewhat speculative matter. And even if we are reassured about the existence of the external world and of other minds, their structure cannot be known without considerable difficulty, since impressions are singular. It seems as if we see causal connections, but how can we be sure?

Pragmatism embraces the sceptical conclusions which follow from the self-dissolution of positivism. A number of writers have of course attempted to re-animate neo-empiricist or moderate conventionalist positions at some point along the slope from classical positivism to pragmatism.[10] But I think it can be shown that these positions are under the same pressure as more classical ones to take either a realist or a pragmatist direction.

Suppose, for example, one argues that what counts in the progress of science is the movement towards theories with greater explanatory power, 'practical adequacy' or whatever. However one specifies a concept of this kind, the basic dilemma remains the same. *Either* it is grounded implicitly in some account of the nature of reality in virtue of which one theory may be better than another *or* such issues are ruled out of court and 'more adequate' simply means something like 'considered preferable by competent members of a given scientific community at a particular time, given the way their discipline is constituted and (perhaps) some more general set of theoretical *interests*'. It is only, I think, in pragmatism that the latter position finds an adequate expression; elsewhere, as for example in van Fraassen's work, it exists in an uneasy relationship with more realist implications.[11]

For the American pragmatist Richard Rorty, the root of the problem is the basic conception of philosophy conceived as a theory of knowledge. His critique is one with which a realist can sympathise, but Rorty moves from denying that *philosophy* has anything specially valuable to say about knowledge, truth etc. to denying that anything much can be said about them *at all*. Rorty's pragmatism is radical because, unlike pragmatists who deconstruct 'truth' in favour of a methodological approach to the justification of knowledge,[12] Rorty finds the whole process of knowledge-justifying somewhat distasteful. It is traditionally associated with 'systematic' philosophy, whereas he prefers to see philosophy as 'edifying', as a 'conversation' which brings together different discourses in a welcoming and non-judgemental spirit.

The same point can be made about pragmatism as I made earlier about realism. It is a philosophical position with a long history, but one which returns to prominence in a specific, new form as a result of the decomposition of empiricism. Unless this decomposition is reversible, there are only two basic alternatives: either the positions variously described as conventionalist, neo-instrumentalist and pragmatist, which dissolve the concept of truth, or those known as rationalist (or transcendentalist) or realist (or materialist) which attempt to sustain it.

As we have seen, the history of empiricist philosophy of science in the twentieth century is basically that of its dissolution[13] or at least its transmutation.[14] This process, which became increasingly clear in the 1960s, gave a new urgency to those who wanted to develop a realist or rationalist alternative. There is a certain parallel with Marxist critiques of capitalism which, even when the world capitalist economy was booming, continued to insist on the fundamental reality of exploitation, the instability of the capitalist form of production, and the inability of non-Marxist economics to theorise it in an adequate manner. But the Marxist critique has seemed more urgent in periods such as the 1930s and the present, when recession and unemployment have cast doubt upon the viability of the capitalist system and the theories which attempt to justify it. Even those who are hostile to the details of the Marxist diagnosis are forced to recognise it as at least a *possible* theory of an all too visible risk of shipwreck, and a *possible* means of escape, rather than a gratuitous and malicious attempt to rock a stably floating boat. In other words, there was something gratuitous, as Popper realised, about asserting a realist position against a background of logical empiricism and its successors; it seems much less gratuitous in a philosophical context heavily influenced by Quine, Kuhn and Feyerabend – to say nothing of the Marxist and 'ecological' criticisms of science as a form of social practice. Modern realist positions are structured by this situation in two related ways. Traditional empiricist theories of perception had been divided between those for which only observations were ultimately real (phenomenalism) and those which claimed that common-sense perception and scientific observation give access to things as they really are (realist empiricism). The latter position had been exploded both as a theory of perception, in a line of argument which goes back to Kant, and as a theory of scientific activity. Secondly, the *rapprochement* between science and philosophy of science meant that the traditional epistemological issues dominant in much philosophy since the seventeenth century were pushed into the background by new advances in the philosophy of language, philosophical logic, and so on. Realist metaphysics in particular distances itself more and more from the epistemological issues which preoccupied earlier realists. In the younger Wilfred Sellars's *Science, Perception and Reality*,[15] for example, there are still several papers of a rather traditional kind on issues to do with perception, although the main thrust of the collection is towards a realism about science and a rejection of the empiricist position that 'what you see is what you get'. It is interesting to note that Sellars's rejection of empiricism is still cast very much in epistemological terms, although the route to real objects is recognised as being through science.

the perceptual world is phenomenal in something like the Kantian sense, the key difference being that the real or 'noumenal' world which supports the 'world of appearances' is not a *metaphysical* world of unknowable things in themselves, but simply the world as constructed by scientific theory.[16]

The rejection of empiricism is the basic trend which marks the distinctiveness of modern realism from earlier variants. There was no way back to the dogma of immaculate perception; a modern realist position had to incorporate the conceptual work of science as it is expressed in complicated redescriptions of phenomena in concepts now recognised to be theory-dependent. Realists believe that something like their philosophical metatheory is required to make sense of scientific activity. And there is a good chance that scientists will explicitly adopt, in some form, a realist position of the kind implicit in their work, though it is also possible for them to fall under the influence of some non-realist philosophy which may or may not affect their practice. The French philosopher and historian of science, Gaston Bachelard, distinguished between the 'diurnal' philosophy presupposed by scientists *in* their work and the 'nocturnal', philosopher's philosophy invoked as a retrospective rationalisation in their private or public reflections *on* their work. In other words, as in other areas of social life, actors can often operate successfully with a false theory or 'consciousness' of what they are doing.

Despite the great diversity of arguments for and against realism, it is possible to see them as combining, in varying degrees, transcendental arguments from the nature of scientific practice and some inductive arguments from the growth of scientific knowledge. The latter construe realism as an empirical hypothesis, confirmed (or at least supported) by the progress of science, and more particularly by the *convergence* of scientific knowledge. What this argument essentially does is to stand on its head an argument sometimes advanced *against* realism. The anti-realist argument goes that, since we are constantly changing our views about the nature of reality, none of the terms with which we attempt to refer to that reality actually do refer successfully. If in Hilary Putnam's example, 'there is nothing in the world which *exactly* fits the Bohr–Rutherford description of an electron', are we to say that Bohr did not refer successfully to electrons? No, says Putnam, because 'there are particles which *approximately* fit Bohr's description'.[17] Bohr's description, though flawed, is not irremediably false, like the concept of phlogiston. But could not all our scientific concepts turn out to be like phlogiston? Clearly they *could* and it is in this sense that realism, on this view, is an empirical hypothesis, but the convergence of scientific knowledge strongly suggests that they will not turn out to be radically off-beam in this way.

The problem with this sort of argument is that while it sounds, to me at least, plausible enough, it is highly vulnerable to sceptical counter-attacks such as those of Mary Hesse, who is unwilling to admit more than what she calls 'the pragmatic criterion': 'the overriding requirement for empirical science to exhibit increasingly successful prediction and hence the possibility of instrumental control of the external world'.[18] Hesse argues that it is a mistake to argue from this instrumental progress (and the accumulation of empirical findings) to theoretical convergence:

> The succession of theories of the atom . . . exhibits no convergence, but oscillates between continuity and discontinuity, field conceptions and particle conceptions, and even speculatively among different typologies of space.[19]

I find this a rather harsh view of the history of science, but it only needs to be a *possible* view in order to cast doubt on the inductivist argument for realism. I shall return at the end of this chapter to discuss how far this argument affects the realist position in general.

The transcendental realist strategy, formally presented by Roy Bhaskar, is anticipated by the intuitions of some earlier philosophers of science. Karl Popper, for example, was uncomfortable with the Viennese position:

> *Logik der Forschung* was the book of a realist but . . . at that time I did not dare to say very much about realism. The reason was that I had not then realised that a metaphysical position, though not testable, might be rationally criticisable or arguable. I had confessed to being a realist, but I had thought that this was no more than a confession of faith.[20]

Realism, for Popper,

> forms a kind of background that gives point to our search for truth. Rational discussion, that is, critical argument in the interest of getting nearer to the truth, a world which we make it our task to discover.[21]

This notion of realism as a philosophy which gives point to, fits in with, or is continuous with science can be found in very many texts (where it is often described as 'scientific realism' to point up this connection).[22] Popper's position has similarities with that of D.-H. Ruben, though Ruben gives the argument a vulgar Marxist twist which would horrify Popper. According to Ruben 'any adequate theory of knowledge must be consistent with science' and this is a strength of Marxist materialism, which he equates with realism: 'our conception of philosophy is one that makes it *continuous* with science, and hence *a posteriori* in character'.[23] Materialism cannot be justified *a priori*, for example by Bhaskar's transcendental arguments from the nature of science. Indeed, such arguments are not necessary: 'to take science as immediate is to take real objects as immediate as well'.[24]

What then is the status of this position? Materialism, says Ruben, is not justifiable *a posteriori*, since idealism is always available as an alternative.[25] But

Although *a posteriori* justification of materialism is not possible, there is still a sense, I think, in which materialism is continuous with the sciences, is an '*a posteriori*' philosophy, whereas idealism is not. It is difficult to specify precisely in what this continuity consists, but it has to do ultimately with unity of approach or outlook. To look at the world materialistically is to look at it in the same sort of way as one looks at it as a scientist. It is a 'diurnal philosophy' which asks us to accept science at its face value, not to move beyond the reality our science attempts to describe for us.[26]

What Ruben ends up with, then, are two statements of faith: (1) in science; (2) in materialism:

(1) . . . what, for us, can make no sense is to ask whether all science and its methodology may be suspect, for there is no Archimedean point lying outside science altogether which would provide any purchase for making such a question intelligible to us. Criticism of science within science does not support the idea of the possibility of a philosophical criticism of all science.[27]

(2) Ultimately, the choice between materialism and idealism is the choice between two competing ideologies. The choice is not an 'epistemological' choice to be made on grounds of stronger evidence or more forceful argument, but a 'political' choice to be made on class allegiance.[28]

Some readers have found the last statement offensive, but it hardly does more than add an *a prioristic* sociology of knowledge to a common-sense realism; the latter may well seem to stand on its own, given the paradoxical flavour of many of the positivist and conventionalist alternatives. If, however, arguments for realism *are* appropriate, the most ambitious available are those developed by Roy Bhaskar, to whose work I now turn.

Bhaskar asks the Kantian question: how is science possible? His answer is that a realist ontology 'is presupposed by the social activity of science'.[29] In other words, for science to be possible or intelligible, the world must be made up of real things and structures:

> that the world is structured and differentiated can be established by philosophical arguments; though the particular structures it contains and the ways in which it is differentiated are matters for substantive scientific investigation.[30]

If we take natural science to be (mainly) a combination of sense perception and experimental activity, the former implies the independent existence of the objects to be perceived. And if this argument proves the independence of experiences and events, a further argument from the nature of experimentation establishes the distinction between sequences of events and causal laws. Experimentation only makes sense if the experimenter is producing the sequence of events but not the causal law which he or she is trying to identify. Since things happen in open systems, the constant conjunctions presupposed by the empiricist account of causation can only be the product of experimental closure: the isolation of the *explanandum* from extraneous influences. Finally, it is part of the nature of a causal law that it obtain in more than one sequence of events: that it be, in Bhaskar's terms, a transfactually active' mechanism grounded in the powers and tendencies of things. *Contra* empiricism, laws are (1) not dependent on empirical regularities (these are neither necessary nor sufficient to establish laws) and (2) not confirmed or falsified by their instances. Instead, they are to be understood as tendencies, interacting with other tendencies such that an observable event may or may not be produced.

What we find in Bhaskar's book is a significantly different conception of philosophy from those examined earlier. In logical positivism, philosophy was 'scientific': it was trimmed to fit a particular conception of science which it then, in turn, trimmed to fit its own norms.[31] It did not and could not offer any specific arguments for realism. On the 'inductivist' argument, too, philosophy is confined to providing a meta-induction from alleged scientific progress. And for Ruben, philosophy is strictly *a posteriori*: in particular, 'there are no non-circular justifications for the belief in a material world'.[32]

For Bhaskar, by contrast, philosophy retains a substantial role as 'under-labourer and occasional midwife' to science. There is however a further question to be answered here: what sort of epistemology or methodology is entailed by the ontological arguments which Bhaskar has developed? Indeed is there *anything* to be said at a general philosophical level about these questions, or should they be left to the sciences?

First, let us look at the relation between ontology and epistemology in the philosophies which Bhaskar criticises. Early in *A Realist Theory of Science* he distinguishes between three broad positions:[33]

1. *Classical empiricism*: 'the ultimate objects of knowledge are atomistic events'.
2. *Transcendental idealism*: 'the objects of scientific knowledge are models, ideals of natural order etc. . . . the natural world becomes a construction of the human mind, or, in its modern versions, of the scientific community'.
3. *Transcendental realism*: 'it regards the objects of knowledge as the structures and mechanisms that generate phenomena; and the knowledge as produced in the social activities of science. These objects are neither phenomena (empiricism) nor human constructs imposed upon the phenomena (idealism) but real structures which endure independently of our knowledge, our experience, and the conditions which allow us access to them.'

From a transcendental realist point of view, classical empiricism and transcendental idealism commit two related errors. They reduce ontology to epistemology, questions about being to questions about our knowledge of being. And in so doing, they also retain an implicit ontology of the 'empirical world'. It is in this sense that Kant called himself an empirical realist as well as a transcendental idealist; in Bhaskar's terminology, empirical realism is common to classical empiricism and to transcendental idealism. One important instance of this is in their analysis of the grounds of causal statements: the experience of constant conjunctions is both necessary and sufficient for the classical empiricist analysis, and necessary but not sufficient for the transcendental idealist. For transcendental realism, by contrast, they are neither necessary nor sufficient.

Bhaskar goes on to develop a conception of scientific discovery in which

1. an effect is identified and described.
2. a hypothetical mechanism is postulated which, *if* it existed, *would* explain the effect.
3. the attempt is made to demonstrate the existence and operation of the mechanism
   (a) positively, by experimental activity, designed to isolate and in some cases directly observe the mechanism.
   (b) negatively, by the elimination of alternative explanations.

To give a favourite realist example: viruses were initially postulated to explain certain diseases for which bacterial agents could not be found; with time, their existence and mode of operation came to be demonstrated. Other postulated mechanisms remain hypothetical: the Freudian unconscious, *if* it exists, *would* have the attractive property of explaining a variety of apparently unconnected psychological phenomena. Even the best possible explanations, however, are in no sense ultimate; there is no 'one true theory', no single way of describing nature which is, in Richard Rorty's ironical phrase, 'Nature's Own'.[34] This is the other side of Bhaskar's distinction between things and descriptions which I quoted at the beginning of this chapter, and his previous page brings out these implications:

> whenever we speak of things or of events etc. in science we must always speak of them and know them under particular descriptions, descriptions which will always be to a greater or lesser extent theoretically determined, which are not neutral reflections of a given world.[35]

This does not at all mean that any theory or explanation is as good as any other; only that there is no philosophical concept of Truth which can provide the ultimate seal for a particular account. Philosophical attempts to turn the semantic concept of truth into an epistemological concept must be replaced by an examination of the ways truth is pursued, ignored etc. in science and ordinary life. To cut short a long discussion of inter-theoretical comparison, we can say that a theory is better than another if it explains (under its descriptions) most of what the second theory explains (under *its* descriptions) plus some further things which are not explained by the second theory.[36] Just what things require explanation is a matter for the science concerned. (To give a trivial example, it is no objection to the Marxist theory of capitalism that it cannot explain, as ethnomethodology can, how to terminate a telephone conversation without offending one's partner.)

There is, of course, a great deal more to be said about, for example, whether the simplicity of a theory or its ability to generate successful predictions is pragmatically important for theory-choice. Realism implies, however, that such criteria should not necessarily be given as much importance as they are, *faute de mieux*, in some positivist and conventionalist theories. On the positivist covering-law model, for example, explanation and prediction are symmetrical: the same law sustains either. But as we have seen, deducibility from a general law is not an explanation, but merely a regularity to be explained by demonstrating the existence and functioning of a mechanism which produces the regularity. And even if we have a pretty good set of *explanatory* mechanisms, as in meteorology or perhaps in the social sciences, the systems may be too open to give us any basis for more than the most tentative predictions.

It is not the purpose of this book to enter the detailed controversies in the philosophy of science literature between realists and anti-realists. Most of these anyway concern realist positions of the kind represented for a time by Putnam. An epistemological realism of this kind is, as we have seen, vulnerable to sceptical attacks based on the history of science. It is, to put it crudely, cowardly at the level of ontology and foolhardy at the level of epistemology. Transcendental realism, by contrast, is ontologically bold and epistemologically cautious: scientific claims must basically be justified within the open-ended practice of science. And science, as Popper realised when he replaced verification with falsification, can never give such claims a permanent right of abode, but merely offer a residence permit until further notice.

Another anti-realist argument which is not pertinent to the transcendental realism defended here is that directed against the 'one true theory', the account of a natural phenomenon which is 'Nature's Own'. As we have seen, Bhaskar is particularly careful to distinguish between human descriptions of reality and the reality which they attempt to describe. All that remains of this anti-realist argument, I think, is a flat rejection of any talk about a reality which is independent of our descriptions of it. But this reference, however displeasing it may be to certain philosophers, is required if scientific activity is to make sense.[37] The same applies to individual references to unobservable entities; it might be nice if all the furniture of the universe were open to direct scientific observation, and all its mechanisms to unambiguous demonstration, but things are not like that.

Finally, it may be worthwhile to ask about the pragmatics of realism. For even if realism is correct, it could be argued that science will develop more flexibly if scientists take a conventionalist view of its assumptions and discoveries, saying of each explanation, that it is *as if* . . . A realist account will be less easy to ignore, and more likely to discourage the making of bold conjectures which conflict with it. I think that there are three mistakes here. First, the sources of dogma in science (whether or not it may be beneficial[38]) are to be found in its social organisation rather than in its metatheory. Secondly, a realist interpretation of a theory puts *more* at stake than does a conventionalist one:

it is only if the working scientist possesses the concept of an ontological realm, distinct from his current claims to knowledge of it, that he can philosophically think out the possibility of a rational criticism of those claims.[39]

Finally, since it seems fairly clear from empirical studies that scientists do in practice shift fairly readily, in the course of their work, back and forth between realistic and conventionalist interpretations, their freedom of movement is actually increased if a realist construal of their work is not blocked off by an anti-realist philosophical dogma (or, for that matter, the twin shibboleths of verifiability and falsifiability). This is the very limited sense in which Feyerabend's 'anything goes' may be a pragmatically useful principle within a scientific community.

To sum up the argument so far, the most important point to be clear about is that, though labels such as empiricism, conventionalism, pragmatism and realism are somewhat arbitrary, and the boundaries between these positions vague and shifting, transcendental realism marks out an underlying opposition which is absolutely fundamental to an understanding of what is at stake in discussions of realism. As we have seen, empiricists, Popperians and pragmatists can be realists in their own way, but their realism is, as Schnädelbach says of Popper, 'methodologically without significance'.[40] Where the basic ontology is one of empirical realism, expressed in the notion of the 'empirical world', or alternatively, where truth-claims are not convertible between theories, the status of the theories remains essentially unchanged, whether or not they are given a formally 'realist' interpretation. What counts, once again, is the underlying movement from empiricism to conventionalism and pragmatism. Once the concepts of science are recognised to be theory-dependent, the only escape from conventionalism is to find some element of necessity, either in the concepts of science or in the objects which they purport to describe. The former strategy is adopted by the position which I am here calling rationalism, expounded with clarity and verve by Martin Hollis and Deryck Beyleveld.[41] This position, though much less fashionable than the realist one, and in my view unsatisfactory, deserves some examination here. This will also, I hope, help in the further clarification of the realist position.

In their modern form, I shall argue, rationalism and realism share a common starting-point. They recognise (*contra* empiricism) the importance of theoretical conceptualisation but insist (*contra* pragmatism) on the need to give these concepts a rational foundation. This is usually expressed in terms of the distinction between nominal (lexical or stipulative) definitions, which merely report or prescribe a verbal usage, and real definitions which make a stronger claim to express some kind of conceptual or natural necessity. The rationalist philosopher Martin Hollis puts it thus:

> I take recent philosophy of science to have shown that empirical judgements presuppose theoretical judgements but not to have

abolished the need for truth in science. Although the danger of a nominalist or conventionalist line on the choice of theoretical terms is thereby stark, it is not clear how a conceptualist line avoids it. It can do so, I submit, only by making old-fashioned claims for the possibility of real definitions.[42]

One way of expressing the difference between realism and rationalism is in terms of the *kinds* of claim they make about real definitions. For rationalism, they most basically express conceptual necessities about the characteristics which we must necessarily attribute to things. Bhaskar's realism cuts out the middle man: real definitions in science are 'fallible attempts to capture in words the real essences of things',[43] i.e. 'their intrinsic structures, atomic constitutions and so on which constitute the real basis of their natural tendencies and causal powers'.[44]

From a realist point of view, then, rationalism is the thesis that we cannot do without the middleman. It is an epistemological thesis compatible with an ontological realism, whereas realism is an ontological thesis with epistemological consequences. For rationalists, ontological realism does not provide a sufficient foundation for our knowledge; it lapses back into pragmatism at the level of epistemology. The argument is essentially that made by Kant in the fourth paralogism (fallacious syllogism) of pure reason. Kant defines his transcendental idealism as

the doctrine that appearances are to be regarded as being, one and all, representations only, not things in themselves and that time and space are therefore only sensible forms of our intuition, not determinations given as existing by themselves, nor conditions of objects viewed as things in themselves. To this idealism there is opposed a *transcendental realism* which regards time and space as something given in themselves, independently of our sensibility. The transcendental realist thus interprets outer appearances (their reality being taken for granted) as things-in-themselves, which exist independently of us and of our sensibility, and which are therefore outside us . . . It is, in fact, this transcendental realist who afterwards plays the part of empirical idealist. After wrongly supposing that objects of the senses, if they are to be external, must have an existence by themselves, and independently of the senses, he finds that, judged from this point of view, all our sensuous representations are inadequate to establish their reality.[45]

Bhaskar's realist response is that Kant is wrong to assume that transcendental realism implies a sceptical position about knowledge. 'Whereas Kant was concerned to analyse the necessary conditions of individual human experience, I am concerned to analyse the necessary conditions of a specific social activity, viz. science . . . a transcendental ontology is necessitated by the *empirical practice* of science.'[46] Once again, this ontology does not give us all the details about what exists and how it works – merely that if science is possible there must be intransitive objects of scientific inquiry which exist and act in certain ways.

The rationalist complaint is that we can only know these intransitive objects of science via a realm of intransitive *theory*, which establishes necessary connections between the concepts of these objects. Without the middleman, the goods will not become available to us. The rationalist wants to make a stronger claim about our theories and a weaker claim about the objects of those theories. Realism demands no middleman other than the scientist, where rationalism wants a further guarantee. 'Only if "knowledge" is understood in an intransitive sense can arguments based on the possibility of knowledge establish categorical conditions for distinguishing genuine from non-genuine science.'[47]

The argument, then is essentially one about the relations between philosophy and science. Rationalists insist on the possibility of intransitive knowledge of conceptually necessary truths, thereby expanding the role of *a priori* knowledge in the sense of knowledge independent of experience because it sets the conditions for possible experience. Beyleveld's critique is important because he spells out an alternative way in which an epistemology might be developed which is at least compatible with a realist ontology. In doing so, he points to a lacuna in realist epistemology, though one which I shall argue is a necessary one, if realist philosophy is to maintain its continuity with science rather than prescribing for it in ways which are both unnecessary and undesirable.

It will be sufficient here to consider two issues: first, Beyleveld's critique of Bhaskar's principle of 'epistemic relativism', and, secondly, their respective analyses of natural necessity. Epistemic relativism is an expression of the general relativity of our knowledge, viz. that whenever we speak of things or events etc. in science we must always speak of them and know them under particular descriptions, descriptions which will always be to a greater or lesser extent theoretically determined, which are not neutral reflections of a given world . . . Philosophers have wanted a theory of truth to provide a criterion or stamp of knowledge. But no such stamp is possible. For the judgement of the truth of a proposition is necessarily intrinsic to the science concerned.[48]

Beyleveld's criticisms of these positions are, as he says, 'fairly standard';[49] they are that the principle of non-contradiction, 'not (*p* and not *p*)' is necessary if we are to know anything, that criteria of 'truth' and 'knowledge' cannot be variable if they are to count as criteria of truth and knowledge. Such principles need to be seen as intransitive and necessary: 'a necessary (epistemological) condition for thought about intransitive objects to be possible'.[50] Some such argument is needed to justify the conclusions allegedly established by Bhaskar's transcendental argument from the nature of science.

This is the point, I think, at which realism can justifiably adopt the sort of arguments traditionally offered by pragmatists, and especially by the refined version of pragmatism developed by Rorty. There is no need for a philosophical theory of truth. The basic intuition of correspondence theories is correct, that statements are true if they correspond to the facts of the matter, but attempts to formalise the notion of correspondence between statements and states of affairs are doomed to failure. Rorty's argument is that

For the pragmatist, the notion of 'truth' as something 'objective' is just a confusion between
(I) Most of the world as it is whatever we think about it (that is, our beliefs have very limited causal efficacy) and
(II) There is something out there in addition to the world called 'the truth about the world' . . .
The pragmatist wholeheartedly assents to (I) – not as an article of faith but simply as a belief that we have never had any reason to doubt – and cannot make sense of (II) when the realist tries to explain (II) with
(III) the truth about the world consists in a relation of

'correspondence' between certain sentences (many of which, no doubt, have yet to be formulated) and the world itself. The pragmatist can only fall back on saying, once again, that many centuries of attempts to explain what 'correspondence' is have failed.[51]

My response, and I think a typical realist response, would be the following:

1. It is not surprising that 'the pragmatist' cannot make sense of (II) above, since it does not seem to make any sense, and realists are certainly not committed to any such principle.
2. Rorty's (III), by contrast, is unproblematic, provided we do not make too much of the notion of 'correspondence'. In a loose sense, it seems to follow from (I), which Rorty accepts, unless one inflates the notion of correspondence to reality in the way which Rorty rightly criticises in philosophical theories of truth-as-correspondence. To avoid such confusions, it is better for realists to drop any commitment to a correspondence theory of truth, but it remains a regulative idea of science, in the strong sense in which science is a meaningless activity unless there is an independent reality (I) for science to describe.

It is precisely his refusal to develop the implications of this latter argument which makes Rorty a pragmatist rather than a realist, but his critique of the notion of correspondence has no dangers for a realist philosophy of science. What science is typically concerned with is not truth or falsity in an absolute and timeless sense, but with relative degrees of truth and falsity, adequacy and inadequacy, better or worse knowledge. It is surely true to say that the sun 'rises' in the east and 'sets' in the west, and certainly truer to say this than to say the opposite, but a better account is one cast in terms of the rotation of the earth. Transcendental realism, as we have seen, must be distinguished from a 'vulgar realist' position that there is some possible description which could encapsulate the Truth about the world. But this is not to say that there is not a 'fact of the matter' which gives meaning to our pursuit of truth.

One way of clarifying this is by looking at the apparently paradoxical formulation of realism in which it is held that all our beliefs about the world could turn out to be false. The answer, I think, has to be that they *could*, right down to the ontological principles established by a transcendental analysis of science. An omnipotent demon could in principle create this illusion, along with all others. This would give a new meaning to human practice, including the practice of science, relativising it to an appearance created by the demon.[52] The interesting questions would then be questions about the causal powers of the demon, though it is not clear who would be around to ask them. Nor shall I. The purpose of this discussion has merely been to show that realism is saying neither as much nor as little as is asserted by some of its critics. Not as much, since it is not committed to the 'one true theory'; not as little, since epistemic relativism does not need to be overcome by a transcendentalist epistemology.

It is not clear, in any case, that transcendentalism can do the job which is required, since its conceptual necessities are little more than redescriptions parasitical upon basic principles of logic and the discoveries of science. Here I shall turn to the comparison of the realist and rationalist accounts of natural necessity.

According to Beyleveld,

> Kantian transcendentalism and transcendental realism share
> (1) the view that the rationality of experimentation, and empirical enquiry generally, requires commitment to intransitive objects; and
> (2) the view that a concept of natural necessity is required to analyse the concept of causality.
> What they disagree about is 'where' natural necessity is to be located or 'how' it is to be analysed.[53]

Bhaskar distinguishes three levels in our knowledge of nature:

1. 'At the *Humean* level a pattern is identified or an invariance is produced.'
2. This is explained by an account of the nature of the thing (x) which produces the effect. 'Now it is contingent that x has the nature (e.g. constitution or structure) that it has. But given that it has, it is necessary that it behaves the way it does . . . . This is the *Lockean* level of knowledge.'
3. 'Now at the third, Leibnizian level possession of that structure or constitution comes to be regarded as defining the kind of thing that x is. Now it is necessary that x has the structure it has if it is to

be the kind of thing it is. It is no longer contingent that hydrogen is a gas with a particular atomic structure; rather anything possessing that structure is hydrogen.'[54]

As Beyleveld shows, the Leibnizian level is basic for rationalism: the Lockean level for realism. References to a thing's liabilities, powers and tendencies are metaphorical for rationalism, literal for realism. Natural necessity is an epistemological category for rationalism; an ontological category for realism. In other words, the rationalist or transcendentalist wishes, for Kantian reasons, to avoid locating natural necessity in the world and to analyse it instead 'as conceptual necessity which resides in intransitive theory, independent of the beliefs of men past, present or future.'[55] But where else, if not in the world, is natural necessity to be located? This, it seems to me, is the crucial objection to Beyleveld's approach. Even if he were right that Bhaskar, by conjoining his analysis of natural necessity with his thesis of epistemic relativism, ends up in an incoherent position which is relativistic *tout court*, it still cannot possibly be right to locate natural necessity in the realm of theory, even (assuming *this* conception can in turn be defended) a realm of theory which is necessarily true. The *concept* of natural necessity, like that of logical necessity, is of course a human creation, but that which makes attributions of natural necessity true or false can only be a state of the world, one which is independent of the contingent emergence of thinking human beings. The Kantian alternative remains perniciously anthropocentric, even when the *anthropos* is given a transcendental status.

One way of supporting the above claims is to address more directly the notion of the natural kinds – for example, animal species – which are defined at the Lockean level. Causal mechanisms are a traditional object of philosophical scepticism, but natural kinds have a more obvious reality, and it is not clear that Beyleveld would want to take a transcendentalist line here.

Finally, however, it should be noted that, even if a rationalist position of this kind is unacceptable as a general epistemology, it may still have an important role to play in the analysis of theories in the natural and human sciences. As Martin Hollis puts it:

there is a class of truths whose denial is impossible, with at least apparent examples in logic, mathematics, formal systems like kinship algebra or neo-Classical micro-economic theory, and perhaps in epistemology or microphysics and, arguably at any rate, in ethics and theology.[56]

In other words, even if we reject Beyleveld's strong claim that all scientific theories, if true, are *a priori* true, this remains the case for much of our theorising in the natural and social sciences. The scope of *a priori* theory in the social sciences, in particular, is something to be discussed in subsequent chapters of this book.

To end this chapter it may be helpful to summarise some of the central themes of realism and its relations with other philosophical traditions. First, it is essentially an ontological doctrine, though it *may* derive support from the growth of scientific knowledge and it strongly suggests,[57] if it does not entail, an optimistic view of the cognitive capacities of human beings. The ontological character of realism means that it shares with neo-pragmatism a critique of the predominantly epistemological stress of much recent philosophy. A further affinity with pragmatism is its naturalistic account of the way in which human social practice, including the practice of science, fits in with the rest of nature; the contrast here is with the empiricist and rationalist stress on the *individual* knowing subject.

Against pragmatism, however, realism insists on the objectivity of ontology. Philosophical ontology shows that there must be intransitive as well as transitive objects of science (things, structures, mechanisms and so forth) and the ontologies of the individual sciences tell us, within the limits of current knowledge, what these are. This is in opposition to logical empiricism and Popperian critical rationalism, which see realism as a metaphysical thesis which either is meaningless or at least cannot be directly argued for. Pragmatists, for their part, may allow a realism of this kind for the same (pragmatic) reasons, or they may confine themselves to a provisional and unproblematic endorsement of the currently accepted *scientific* ontologies. Rationalism, finally, may include a qualified acceptance of a realist ontology, but insists on combining this with a special theory of our knowledge of its objects.

The distinction between the domains of the real, the actual and the empirical forms the basis of the realist critique of the empiricist doctrine of the 'actuality' of causal laws (i.e. that they hold between events or states of affairs).[58] This, as Bhaskar shows, generalises from the special case of closed systems and thus 'prevents the question of the conditions under which experience is in fact significant in science from being posed'.[59] By demonstrating the reality of causal mechanisms, realism also subverts the conventionalist and pragmatist view that they are merely imagined, and the rationalist position that they are imagined but also necessary. More generally, realism agrees about the importance of the empirical movement in science but denies the 'empirical realist' ontology to which the other positions adhere. Here we come back to our starting-point, with the recognition that the 'epistemic fallacy', the attempt to analyse being in terms of our knowledge of being, merely creates an implicit ontology of its own.

On the relation between science and philosophy, realism adopts an intermediate position between the anti-philosophical philosophy of the pragmatists and the rationalist conception of philosophy as the judge of science. Empiricist, conventionalist and pragmatist philosophies all claimed to be philosophies *for* science, but empiricism was too restrictive, and conventionalism and pragmatism too tolerant, for the guidance they offered to be of much help. Most of the time, their main use was as anti-weapon weapons; one position could be used to neutralise the restrictive prescriptions of another.

How far might this be said for realism too? I think that its contribution is indeed in large part a negative one, since it is a position which, I have argued, comes naturally to scientists except when they are either very unsure of their ground in a particular domain or are trying to fit their practice into a set of over-refined philosophical categories. These two conditions, however, describe fairly well the endemic state of the social sciences, which thus represent, in my view, one area of science among others (another candidate might be microphysics) where a realist approach is sufficiently controversial to raise a set of interesting fundamental issues. In the following chapter I shall discuss the implications of a realist metatheory for the contemporary social sciences.

3

Realism and Social Science

What are the implications of the approach outlined in the previous chapter for the practice of social research? We can begin to answer this question by reviewing some of the realist principles which have already been mentioned. In the sphere of ontology, we have:

1. The distinction between transitive and intransitive objects of science: between our concepts, models etc. and the real entities, relations and so forth which make up the natural and the social world.

2. The further stratification of reality into the domains of the real, the actual and the empirical. The last of these is in a contingent relation to the other two; to be (either for an entity or structure or for an event) is *not* to be perceived.

3. The conception of causal relations as tendencies, grounded in the interactions of generative mechanisms; these interactions may or may not produce events which in turn may or may not be observed.

4. In addition to these three ontological claims, and related to the first one, we have the rejection of both empiricism and conventionalism above. The practical expression of this epistemological position is the concept of real definition. Real definitions, which are important for both realist and rationalist philosophies of science, are neither summaries of existing verbal usage nor stipulations that we should use a term in a particular way. Although they are of course expressed in words, they are statements about the basic nature of some entity or structure. Thus a real definition of water would be that its molecules are composed of two atoms of hydrogen and one of oxygen. This human discovery about water comes to be expressed as a definitional property of it.

5. Finally, and related to (3) above, the realist conception of explanation involves the postulation of explanatory mechanisms and the attempt to demonstrate their existence.

In considering the implications of these principles for the social sciences, it is essential to bear in mind the distinction between a philosophical and a scientific ontology. A philosophical ontology of the kind outlined here does not tell us what the structures, entities and mechanisms which make up the world actually are; this is a matter for the individual sciences. In the case of the social sciences, for example, a realist metatheory will not, of itself, enable us to choose between a conception which confines itself to the study of individual actions and one which casts its explanations in terms of larger social structures.

What we first need to ask, then, is what account of social reality would *rule out* a realist programme of the kind outlined above. Broadly speaking, realism will be inapplicable if there are:

(a) no intransitive objects of social science, no objects susceptible of real definition and
(b) nothing capable of being explained in terms of generative mechanisms.

Let us take (a) first. Intransitivity, it will be recalled, means essentially that 'things exist and act independently of our descriptions',[1] where 'our' refers to human beings in general. It seems fairly clear that this principle needs to be modified in the case of human actions and social structures, where the agents' conceptions are not external to the facts described but make up part at least of the reality of those facts. A quarrel, for example, cannot adequately be described except with reference to the participants' perceptions of their situation as one of hostility. If they do not perceive the situation in this way, they are merely simulating a quarrel. Quarrelling, in other words, is 'concept-dependent' for the participants in a way in which the collision of two asteroids or two sub-atomic particles is not.

This concept-dependence of social phenomena does not however rule out their intransitivity. The First World War, or the Sino-Soviet rift of the late 1950s were as they were independently of anything I write about them today. What the anti-realist requires is a more radical argument which denies that there is any fact of the matter about such matters. The most plausible way to make such an argument is to say something like this:

1. Social situations do not exist independently of the way they are interpreted by those involved in them or by outside observers.
2. Such interpretations are essentially arbitrary.

This argument is not of course essentially different from a radical conventionalism about the natural world. What needs to be explained is its apparently greater plausibility as an account of the social. Let us take three assertions about 'society':

1. Society is not observable.
2. Society is theoretical.
3. Any assertion about society is as good as any other.

The first must clearly be accepted. We can of course study a national community or a group by observing what goes on, asking questions, etc., but there is no such thing as observing a society *as such*. The limits of French society are not the state frontiers of France, not only because France has territories and influence elsewhere in the world but because 'French society' is a theoretical concept, where 'theoretical' means something more than just unobservable. The best way of illustrating this is by looking at the history of the term 'society' and the different ways in which it has been used since, roughly, the eighteenth century.

In other words, to talk about a collection of people, in one or more geographical sites, with various forms of material equipment etc. as a *'society'* is to enter a particular language-game which licences some theoretical moves and not others, and in particular introduces an element of abstraction.

Now a residual element of truth in empiricism is that the use of abstract or theoretical terms has to be legitimated in a way in which a 'lower-level' vocabulary does not. The modern concept of society, for instance, had to be squeezed into some of the conceptual space occupied by the earlier and somewhat more concrete term 'state'.[2] The early resistance to its introduction was fairly obviously political: the term 'society' was seen as in some way linked with the third estate and potentially threatening to the state. In our time this political hostility to the concept of society generally takes the form of individualism: 'the individual and society'. But this ethical or political individualism is only one aspect of an approach whose sharpest theoretical tool is the reductionist thesis of 'methodological individualism'. Talk of society, or of social wholes in general, it is claimed, is only a shorthand or summary redescription of something which must ultimately be described and explained in terms of individual action. As J. S. Mill put it, 'the laws of the phenomena of society are, and can be, nothing but the actions and passions of human beings united together in the social state'.[3] But can we in fact do without a concept of society? As we have seen, the most favoured alternative is an ontology of individual persons and their actions, where social structures are merely summary, metaphorical redescriptions of these. The advantage is that the identity criteria of people are given unproblematically by their bodies, which are almost always clearly distinct from other bodies. It turns out, however, that this does not get us very far, because the more interesting human actions are those which presuppose a network of social relations. And if these social relations are a precondition of individual actions, it seems odd to think of them as any less real than those actions.

What is true, of course, is that we are not sure how to characterise these relations and that our characterisations will be tentative, relative to particular explanatory purposes, and so forth. But this does not mean that some set of real social relations is not a necessary condition for all but the most banal human actions. I can pick my nose all by myself, but I cannot cash cheques, write books, or declare war.

What needs to be explained is why most people in our society will take on trust any confidently presented assertion about, say, the structure of DNA, but will look sceptically at an assertion about the social structure of modern Britain – and why they are right to do so. To say that biochemistry is a 'mature' science, and that sociology is not, is not very helpful. References to accuracy of measurement are also somewhat beside the point. The problem is not that we cannot make precise measurements in the social sciences but that we are not sure what purpose they serve, since the interesting explanatory structures, and even their *explananda*, seem irremediably opaque.

Considerations like these may seem to point towards a conventionalist account of the social sciences, in which all their significant terms are surrounded by scare quotes and all their assertions preceded by an implicit 'everything takes place as if'.[4] Yet this is to concede too much to the sceptics. There are some effects, such as the tendency for the social position of parents to influence the educational achievements of their children, which are as real and general as one could reasonably expect, though of course we still need to investigate the mechanisms which produce these effects. The fact that processes of interpretation underlie all these terms as well as our postulated explanations of the links between them does not rule out a realist construal of these theories. Instead, as I shall argue later in this chapter, it suggests that we should recognise that the social sciences are more closely related to common-sense thinking than are the natural sciences; they do not so much provide radically new knowledge as more adequate formulations of our intuitions about social affairs.

We have seen, then, that the question of intransitive objects of social science turns out to be essentially a question about the scope and implications of interpretation in this domain. I have sketched out an argument to the effect that even if the building-bricks of social science are 'interpreted' building-bricks in a more radical and far-reaching sense than are the component parts of natural scientific theories, and even if the structures postulated within the social sciences tend to be presented, for good reasons, in a tentative way, this does not prevent us asking questions of a realist kind about these structures. In a moment I shall look more closely at the idea that the elementary structures of society are not just interpreted, but are *nothing but interpretations*. But even if this radical interpretivist position could be sustained, it still would not follow without further argument that there were no criteria for judging interpretations.

Before directly addressing these issues, let me deal rapidly with (b) above, the question whether there is anything in the social world which can be explained in realist terms by generative mechanisms. This of course depends on (a) above, since if we cannot even specify the explananda in the social sciences there is not much point in looking for explanatory mechanisms. And depending what we admit as explananda, the types of mechanism will presumably vary too: it would be odd if system equilibrium could be explained in just the same way as individual choice.

As with (a) above, the most radical version of (b) takes the form of the recommendation that the social sciences should confine themselves to the study of individual action. It can then be argued, in either hermeneutic or rationalist terms, that the explanation of human actions in terms of the actors' reasons for acting is something distinct from causal explanation. Part of the appeal of this claim has derived from the obvious inapplicability of the empiricist analysis of causality in terms of the constant conjunction of logically independent events. My reasons for making a cup of coffee (to revive myself, to relieve my thirst, to have a break from writing, etc.) are not logically independent of my doing so. Even if my fatigue does not cause me to drink a cup of coffee, in the directly physical sense in which it might cause me to fall asleep over my manuscript, it can surely contribute to the reasons for my coffee-drinking, as part of a complex concatenation of physical and mental states. And there seems no reason why the realist concept of mechanism should not stretch over all these conditions. Even if one wants, as Rom Harré does, to deny that reasons are causes, one can still argue (as Harré and Secord do) that reason-explanations are the analogues of mechanism-explanations in the natural sciences. In other words, whatever view one adopts on the reasons/causes issue, a realist interpretation can be given of the resultant explanatory models.[5]

In my view, 'the real reason' for an action is best understood as the reason which was causally efficacious in producing that action, but the realist analysis will work, I think, equally well for a rationalist who defines 'real' in this context as something like 'rationally compelling' and, like Martin Hollis, holds that 'rational action is its own explanation'.[6]

It seems, then, that questions about the applicability of realism in the social sciences will turn essentially around the first of the questions raised in this chapter: the existence of intransitive objects of social science. I shall therefore outline (1) Roy Bhaskar's arguments for naturalism, and intransitivity; (2) Ted Benton's criticism that his position is not naturalistic enough and (3) Rom Harré's alternative, anti-naturalist conception of social being.

First, we need to get clear what is at stake in debates over naturalism. As we saw in Chapter 1, the logical positivist thesis of unified science made strong claims for the unity of the laws of science or of the language of science, based on a physicalist reductionism. The contemporary debates focus instead around the weaker claim of a methodological unity of science, in the sense that the methods of the natural sciences can, in general, be applied to the social sciences or; as Bhaskar puts it, 'that it is possible to give an account of science under which the proper and more-or-less specific methods of both the natural sciences and social sciences can fall'. Naturalism in this sense 'does not deny that there are significant differences in these methods grounded in real differences in their subject matters and in the relationships in which their sciences stand to them'.[7] What it claims is that a realist interpretation can meaningfully be given to social scientific knowledge.

Bhaskar starts from the question: 'What properties do societies possess that might make them possible objects of knowledge for us?'[8] He argues, in the way summarised at the beginning of this chapter, 'that societies are irreducible to people', 'that social forms are a necessary condition for any intentional act,[9] that their *pre-existence* establishes their *autonomy* as possible objects of scientific investigation and that their *causal power* establishes their reality'. This in turn entails a 'transformational model of social activity': 'Society is both the ever-present *condition* (material cause) and the continually reproduced *outcome* of human agency.'

> The conception I am proposing is that people, in their conscious activity, for the most part unconsciously reproduce (and occasionally transform) the structures governing their substantive activities of production. Thus people do not marry to reproduce the nuclear family or to work to sustain the capitalist economy. Yet it is nevertheless the unintended consequence (and inexorable result) of, as it is also a necessary condition for, their activity.[10]

This in turn entails a relational conception of the subject matter of the social sciences, in which the practices of agents take place within a set of structurally (and hence relationally) defined positions.[11] Where these relations are part of the definition of the relata, as in buyer/seller; they will be termed internal relations; where they are contingent (e.g. shopper/traffic warden), they are external relations.

This abstract model of social reality, which of course displays strong similarities with other contemporary specifications of the relation between action and structure,[12] is clearly compatible with wide variations in the degree to which particular actions are structured. It does not take the expertise of a labour lawyer to notice that the contractual obligations of an academic are very different from those of the majority of workers. A more interesting, and less determinate area of controversy arises between those who stress the essentially voluntary character of all human actions and those who emphasise structural constraints (which may of course be enabling as well as constraining in a narrow sense). There are powerful currents in textual interpretation, for example, which would analyse this book as the more or less automatic product of a set of theoretical and ideological structures, plus a residual category of authorial desire and a few other material conditions.

It is perhaps not appropriate for me, as author, to address this hyperstructuralist conception; all that is required here is to point out that it still logically requires some notion of agency to make the structures work. Sceptical doubts about the possibility of social science take the opposite tack of questioning the reality and efficacy of social structures. Rom Harré, in his brilliant book *Social Being*, seems to flirt with this view, by confining his attention to structures-of-action as the object of social psychology, conceived in non-naturalistic terms:

> The fact that both natural and social sciences use models in the same way may suggest misleadingly that they share a common epistemology. The differences emerge when we compare the relation of fact to theory in each kind of science. In the social sciences facts, *at the level at which we experience them*, are wholly the creation of theorizing, of interpreting. Realists in social science hold, and I would share their belief, that there are global patterns in the behaviour of men in groups, though as I have argued we have no adequate inductive method of finding them out.[13]

Harré's strategy, in a nutshell, is to bracket out a noumenal realm of latent structures and to confine his research programme in social psychology to structures as they are perceived by actors. Role, he plausibly suggests, 'is experienced, not as a relational property in which the individual stands to the collectives of which he or she is a member, but rather as a systematic set of psychological and microsocial imperatives and constraints'.[14] This, I think, is true and important, but to stress the latter conception of role is not to imply that the former is in some way inaccessible, even (!) to actors. A whole series of techniques, from organisational design to transactional analysis is aimed precisely at explicating the former conception. Indeed if socialisation is to mean something more than behaviour modification, it can only be the inculcation of structural conceptions of this kind. To teach a child that it should not make excessive noise is to give it a conception of an environment made up of other people who are the bearers of rights to a reasonable degree of peace and quiet. I am not sure that Harré would want to question any of this, but his discussion constantly points towards a distinction between an empirically oriented ethogenic social psychology and an inevitably speculative sociology. And the rationale for any such distinction remains unclear.

What does emerge, I think, from this discussion, is that we must look more closely at the relations between social structures and the activities they govern. Roy Bhaskar suggests three 'ontological limitations on a possible naturalism':

(1) Social structures, unlike natural structures, do not exist independently of the activities they govern;

(2) Social structures, unlike natural structures, do not exist independently of the agents' conceptions of what they are doing in their activity;

(3) Social structures, unlike natural structures, may be only relatively enduring (so that the tendencies they ground may not be universal in the sense of space–time invariant).[15]

These qualifications are, I think, on the right lines, but they must themselves be qualified in ways suggested by some criticisms made by Ted Benton.[16] The third principle is of limited relevance and can be dealt with fairly swiftly. As Benton points out, it does not mark out a sharp dividing line between natural and social structures, since many natural structures are also only relatively enduring. All that is required for social science to be possible is that social structures be sufficiently enduring for their examination to be feasible and worthwhile. And even the most radical proponents of the view that only synchronic investigation is possible in the social sciences always allow themselves time at least to carry out their investigations. If there is a problem about social structures, it is surely not their mutability *per se* but their general messiness and fluidity.

Bhaskar's first principle of differentiation seems to require little more than a bit of tinkering to render it acceptable. First, it must be counterfactualised, such that the reference includes *possible* actions governed by the structure (e.g. a power structure). These may be negative possible actions, as in deterrence. Secondly, it must be noted that the activities which sustain a structure are not always identical with those which it governs in its functioning. A structure of gift exchange does not exist independently of the giving of gifts, but it also presupposes the possession or acquisition of potential gifts (whether or not these are possessed or acquired under that description).

Bhaskar's second principle also requires some clarification, but even when clarified it points further to the central issue which is at stake between naturalism and anti-naturalism. First, we should note that agency itself requires that the agents have *some* conception of what they are doing; sleepwalking is only a marginal case of action. Conversely, this conception need not be correct for the action to be successful, and in some cases a correct conception of the activity will render it impossible; I can mislead you deliberately or unintentionally, but not if you perceive me to be misleading you. More broadly, agents need not be conscious of their implication in structures such as that of the capitalist economy, which nevertheless govern their actions; other structures get their efficacy from their imaginary power as slogans. Ideologies will tend to contain a mixture of conscious and unconscious beliefs, and this may be an important part of their power.

It will be helpful here to refer to Bhaskar's distinction between causal interdependence (between social structures and human representations of them) on the one hand, and existential intransitivity 'which is an a priori condition of investigation and applies in the same way in the social, as the natural sphere'. Both principles are required for realist social science, as against positivism which neglects interdependence and hermeneutic theories which 'dissolve intransitivity'.[17] Hermeneutics is right however to draw attention to the central importance of meanings for the social sciences, and to the fact that they have to be understood, not simply registered or measured. To this must be added the practical difficulties of measurement and empirical testing in the social sciences: the virtual unavailability of experimentation and closure, the irreversibility of most social processes, etc.[18] Here we can see that certain consequences, such as the impossibility of prediction, do not vitiate a realist conception of social science as they would one which was positivistically conceived.

Behind all this, however, is the fundamental issue, briefly raised at the beginning of this chapter, of the relation between the social sciences and common-sense social knowledge. This issue is conceived in very different ways in different theories about the social and natural sciences,[19] but what seems to emerge fairly clearly is that the social sciences remain closer to commonsense thinking, which is anyway more pervasive and powerful in the social world. By this I mean that we have intuitions about the structure of almost all the social processes we may care to think about; these may be right or wrong, but they at least give us an *entrée* into the subject matter. In physical reality, by contrast, we have intuitions only about a restricted range of phenomena – billiard balls but not particles, chairs but not molecular structures, people and animals but not bacteria and viruses, and so on. In crude terms, the social sciences begin with a head-start over the natural sciences, but instead of running straight ahead in pursuit of new knowledge they move around in small circles and spend a lot of time re-inspecting the starting-block.[20]

One diagnosis of this situation is to say that social scientists are too ambitious in their speculations, that they try to run before they can walk. This is probably true of all science; the difference, I think, for the social sciences is that they *cannot* really walk; a better metaphor is a bicycle, which is easy to ride at 10 m.p.h. and impossible at 2. It is of course possible to replicate standardised tests *ad nauseam*, but replication makes little difference to the acceptance or rejection of the results previously obtained; these tend to be accepted or rejected on more global theoretical principles.

One has to recognise the utopianism in the nineteenth-century aspiration that the social sciences would produce 'the same kind of sensational illumination and explanatory power already yielded up by the sciences of nature'.[21] Social science is not without surprises, but the important ones are arguably not the findings which go against our expectations, but the qualitative discovery of new ways of conceiving social reality – ways which are however still in some sense continuous with common-sense perceptions. Social science, it seems, is necessarily tentative, theoretically pluralistic, and incomplete.

The other side of this coin, however, is that common-sense descriptions of social phenomena can and must be taken as a starting-point in social scientific theorising. *Can*, because they provide the beginnings of definitions of the phenomena and thus help in the otherwise bewildering activity of object-constitution or, in Goldmann's term, *découpage*,[22] 'given the mish-mash nature of social reality'.[23] *Must*, because however imperfect they may be, to the extent that they are the perceptions of agents involved in that situation they will influence the very nature of that situation. This is the (partial) truth of W. I. Thomas's famous claim that 'If men define situations as real they are real in their consequences.'[24] The extent to which this is true, as I suggested earlier, will depend on the specific features of a given social situation.

It can now be seen that the concept-dependence and activity-dependence of social structures appears not so much as an obstacle but as a resource in social theorising. We can ask, in other words, what a given society must be like in order for people to behave within it, and to conceive it, in the ways they do. (Here, as Bhaskar notes,[25] there is a partial analogy with philosophical investigations into the transcendental presuppositions of an empirically identified activity, such as that of scientific practice.) As I shall suggest in more detail in Chapter 6, a good example of this process of theorising is Marx's *Capital*, conceived simultaneously as an investigation into the mechanisms of the capitalist mode of production and a critique of its representations in common-sense conceptions and in the theories of classical political economy.[26] This mode of enquiry is not however peculiar to Marx, whose philosophical orientation is close to transcendental realism;[27] it can also be found, in a neo-Kantian framework, in much of classical sociology, e.g. in the work of Durkheim and Max Weber.[28]

It is now time to summarise this outline of a realist strategy in the social sciences, which will serve as a basis for the more detailed discussions in subsequent chapters. The notion of real definition serves as a leitmotif to the practice of social research on a realist basis. The social scientist directs his or her attention to an object of inquiry which is already defined in certain ways in the world of everyday life and ordinary language. (This is of course true of natural objects as well, but with the important difference that natural objects do not have concepts of what they are doing when they fall, collide, melt, die and so forth.) The social scientist will typically seek to redescribe this object so as to bring out its complexity, the way in which it is determined by its internal and external environment as an outcome of a multiplicity of interacting tendencies.

The conception of the object of inquiry will crucially determine the sorts of method which are appropriate to its investigation. The ethnomethodological approach of conversational analysis will not help us to understand the rate of profit in a capitalist economy, nor will the law of value explain how one can terminate a telephone conversation without embarrassment. Historical analysis may or may not be relevant to the study of a particular contemporary situation. In other words, the question of what is needed to explain an observable social phenomenon will receive a contextually specific answer.

In this redefinition of objects of social inquiry and prior to any choice of methods of investigation, are questions of social ontology. What sort of object are we trying to describe and explain? To what extent is it a product of the interpretations of human beings, and to what extent is it structured by 'deeper causes which are opaque to human consciousness'.[29] Now arguments can be made, by realists as by anyone else, about these perennial disputes within social ontology, but they are not, I think, specifically realist arguments. In other words, they concern the nature of human societies rather than the nature of social scientific theories.

Rom Harré, who has argued for an interactionist, interpretivist social psychology, and Roy Bhaskar, who has upheld a more structuralist and materialist approach in the social sciences, can both legitimately construe their proposals in realist terms. Both can claim to be propounding ways of getting at the fundamental structures and generative mechanisms of social life: where they differ is in their accounts of the constitution of social reality and of how this reality can be known.[30] Realism does not uniquely license either of these approaches. What it *does* provide, however, is a framework in which these alternative social ontologies can be rationally compared and discussed – in which they are not brushed aside, as in the positivist and conventionalist traditions, as 'mere' definitional assumptions.

Realist philosophies of science, as we have seen, abandon a number of positivist assumptions about scientific theorising. The most important of these are probably the theory-observation distinction and the covering-law model of explanation, which are replaced, respectively, by the idea of a complex network of relatively 'theoretical' and relatively 'observational' statements and by the idea of explanation as the attempt to represent the generative mechanisms which bring about the *explanandum*. A corollary of the latter principle is that explanation is not identified with prediction, the latter being possible, strictly speaking, only where the system is closed by natural or experimental means. For practical purposes in the social sciences we can forget about closures, so that any predictions we make will be necessarily tentative and will not provide decisive tests of our theories.

If, then, the criteria of theory-choice in the social sciences are purely explanatory, how are we to judge explanations? It will be remembered that the realist model of explanation involves three basic steps, the postulation of a possible mechanism, the attempt to collect evidence for or against its existence, and the elimination of possible alternatives. We shall therefore feel we have a good explanation if

1. the postulated mechanism is capable of explaining the phenomena;
2. we have good reason to believe in its existence;
3. we cannot think of any equally good alternatives.

So far so good, but this abstract model does not help in the characteristic situation in the social sciences in which we are expected to choose between several alternative theories and their associated mechanisms and where the object of inquiry is complex and over-determined. Any guidelines will be necessarily vague, but I think that the following principles are not entirely trivial. First, we should not be afraid of theoretical abstraction, since 'observational' statements have no special privilege in this framework. Entities are not to be multiplied unnecessarily, but nor are they to be excluded for being unobservable. Second, the realist emphasis on the stratification of reality should make us aware of the need to fit particular explanations within a wider context. This does not mean that the social totality needs to be invoked to explain the most microscopic social event, but it does mean, for example, that micro-economic theories should connect up with propositions about economic systems and their reproduction, and are inadequate to the extent that they do not.[31] In other words, and this may be counted as a third principle, *a priori* considerations of this kind have a part to play in the evaluation of social theories. I have already discussed some apparently *a priori* constraints on social theories of the relation between agency and social structure, although it emerged that the precise form of their interrelations was a matter for empirical determination in each case.

I do not think one can go far beyond these very general principles. Where two or more theories score equally well according to all these criteria, there seem to be no general grounds for rational preference. Simplicity is an obvious candidate, but a preference for simplicity in all cases cannot be justified once one abandons conventionalist positions for which it is pretty well the only available criterion. There is however something of importance behind discussions of simplicity: namely, the idea that choices thus governed maximise the speed of scientific advance by making theories more easily testable. I do not here want to go into the question whether the choice in all cases of the simpler theory *does* in fact have these beneficial consequences, but merely to uphold the underlying principle, that theories should be adopted which on the whole maximise the chances of further intertheoretical debate within the sciences concerned. In other words, we should adopt, other things being equal, theories which are open in this way, rather than, say, reductionist theories, which close off discussion within one level even if they promise to reopen it at another.

The slogan, then, is 'keep them talking'. Once again, it might be thought that this *desideratum* would be best satisfied by conventionalist metatheories. This however seems not to be the case if we recall that the 'talking' necessarily includes the rational critique of existing theories, and it is precisely conventionalism which tends to block off theoretical criticism with its doctrine of the arbitrariness of 'definitional questions'. Once again, it needs to be stressed that the most powerful reason for adopting a realist metatheory is to acquire a framework for the rational discussion of ontological questions.

This principle of dialogue-preservation may be relevant to theory-choice in a further way. It has been suggested, by Mary Hesse and others, that in those cases, particularly frequent in the social sciences, in which there are no clear scientific grounds for the choice between two or more theories, it may be legitimate to choose on grounds of general social values.[32] And among such values, the maximisation of serious discussion might well be argued to have a special place, for the Habermasian reason that it may be a condition for consensus on central issues of truth and justice.

The realist emphasis on the legitimacy and importance of theoretical argument should not be understood to imply the depreciation of empirical research. What it does suggest, I think, is that such research cannot achieve useful results in the absence of theoretical reflection on the structuration of empirical data and a rejection of empiricism, understood as an exclusive focus on social phenomena which are empirically observable and measurable. As Bhaskar puts it,

the *conceptual* aspect of the subject matter of the social sciences circumscribes the possibility of measurement. . . . For meanings cannot be measured, only understood. Hypotheses about them must be expressed in language, and confirmed in dialogue. Language here stands to the conceptual aspect of social science as geometry stands to physics. And precision in meaning now assumes the place of accuracy in measurement as the a posteriori arbiter of theory. It should be stressed that in both cases theories may continue to be justified and validly used to explain, even though *significant* measurement of the phenomena of which they treat has become impossible.[33]

The upshot, I think, is that a realist strategy for the social sciences needs to engage in a detailed way with the conceptions of interpretation which have been worked out within the frameworks of hermeneutics and critical theory. The following chapters are devoted to this task.

4

Realism and Hermeneutics

This chapter and Chapter 5 are intended to form a unit, since the relations between hermeneutics and critical theory are extremely close, though also very complex. First, it is worth noting that it was Jürgen Habermas's development of critical theory which introduced the term 'hermeneutics' into the social scientific culture of the English-speaking world. One of Habermas's central preoccupations has always been the issue of 'methodological dualism' in the social sciences and the fact that they are 'pervaded by the opposition between different approaches and aims.'[1] And, given his intellectual background, it was only natural that he should discuss these issues in relation to the German hermeneutic tradition and its most prominent contemporary representative, Hans-Georg Gadamer. Though Habermas's massive synthesis has a number of other intellectual sources, most notably of course the earlier generation of critical theorists, it is not impossible to see it as one variant among others of 'critical hermeneutics'.[2]

There are of course non-Habermasian ways of defending a hermeneutic and anti-naturalistic view of the social sciences, but his attempt to develop an alternative conception, beyond positivism and hermeneutics, is in my view one of the most appealing strands in contemporary social theory, and one which poses crucially important questions to the programme of realist naturalism. It was Habermas, more than anyone else, who brought *Verstehende* sociology out of the ghetto (in which it was seen as one option among others), and showed how hermeneutic issues needed to be put at the starting-point of social theory. Giddens and others have drawn these conclusions, with the result that the initial conditions of social theorising have come to look very different from the way they looked in the 1950s and 1960s. This is, I admit, a highly partial view of the contemporary sociological scene, but if I am right, it is here that we find the central questions for a realist philosophy of the social sciences.

As we saw in Chapter 1, the term 'hermeneutics' has been used since the eighteenth century to refer to the interpretation of texts. Initially restricted to religious writings, it was gradually extended to classical philology and to linguistic understanding in general. Understanding was in turn seen as the foundation of the human sciences, notably by Wilhelm Dilthey (1833–1911). Dilthey's distinction between the sciences of nature and those of the mind or spirit (*Geist*), and the concomitant distinction between explanation and understanding, had an enormous influence in the German-speaking countries.

An even broader conception of hermeneutics, which derives from Heidegger's *Being and Time* (1927), was made popular in the 1960s by Hans-Georg Gadamer.[3] Hermeneutics is universal because understanding is the fundamental way in which human beings participate in the world. Finally, the term has come to be used in a derivative way to refer to those variants of social theory which give a special place to understand or *Verstehen*: symbolic interactionism, phenomenological sociology, ethnomethodology and so on.

It may be helpful, therefore, to distinguish a general (or universal) and a special hermeneutic thesis. The general thesis, represented by Gadamer, stresses the hermeneutic starting point which precedes and underlies any scientific inquiry; the special thesis argues (instead or as well) for a specific hermeneutic dimension in some of the sciences, implying for example a commitment to a *Verstehende* sociology.

Gadamer, for example, undoubtedly accepts the special thesis as it applies to the human sciences, but his main concern is to argue the general thesis.

> Understanding . . . shows the universality of human linguisticality as a limitless medium that carries everything, not only the culture that has been handed down through language, but absolutely everything, because everything is incorporated into the realm of understandability in which we interact.[4]

His view of the sciences is broadly that of Husserl's *Crisis of the European Sciences* and Heidegger's *Being and Time*.[5] It forms the starting point for another essay on 'The Universality of the Hermeneutic Problem':

> the central question of the modern age . . . is . . . how our natural view of the world – the experience of the world that we have as we simply live out our lives – is related to the unassailable and anonymous authority that confronts us in the pronouncements of science.[6]

Hermeneutic reflection, like Husserl's transcendental phenomenology, is supposed to mediate between science and the life-world, and in particular between their respective languages. It was 'the specific merit and the specific weakness' of Greek science that it 'originated in the linguistic experience of the world. In order to overcome this weakness, its naive anthropocentrism, modern science has also renounced its merit, namely its place in the natural attitude of man to the world.'[7] Hermeneutic reflection, then, forms a bridge between the special sciences and the life-world, making explicit the presuppositions of the sciences, their forms of abstraction, and, most of all, their guiding concept of *method*. Gadamer puts it in Wittgensteinian terms: 'The language games of science remain related to the metalanguage presented in the mother tongue.'[8]

All this must I think be accepted. Despite the vagueness of Gadamer's concept of the natural attitude to the world, it marks out an important area of enquiry: that of world-pictures, ideas of natural order, and so forth.[9] But what about the social and human sciences? It is interesting to note that Gadamer does not assimilate the social sciences to the human sciences or *Geisteswissenschaften*: philology, literary criticism, aesthetics, cultural history, etc. Instead, he draws a fairly conventional distinction between the natural sciences and the *Geisteswissenschaften*,[10] and then locates the social sciences somewhere in the middle. The essay cited above continues with the argument that the separation or alienation of science from our natural experience of the world is

> without importance for the natural sciences as such. The true natural scientist knows how very particular is the realm of knowledge of his science in relation to the whole of reality . . . .
> The so-called humanities (Humaniora) still relate easily to the

common consciousness, so far as they reach it at all, since their objects belong immediately to the cultural tradition and the traditional education system. But the modern social sciences stand in a peculiarly tense relationship to their object, a relationship which especially requires hermeneutical reflection. For the methodical alienation to which the social sciences owe their progress is related here to the human-societal world.[11]

Gadamer's view of the social sciences, so far as it can be disentangled from his more specific disagreements with Habermas,[12] is that they should indeed be conscious of the 'hermeneutic conditions' which apply to the *Verstehende Geisteswissenschaften*' and their implications for the practice of social science. He notes that (some of the time?) the social sciences do not aim at understanding but rather 'incorporate linguistically sedimented truisms in their attempt to capture the real structure of society.' And even if they do aim at understanding, they are committed, *qua* sciences, to a methodically alienated form of understanding, which therefore requires further hermeneutic reflection.[13]

What then are the hermeneutic conditions which govern the *Geisteswissenschaften* and, whether or not they heed them, the social sciences as well? Gadamer's hermeneutic philosophy is concerned with the sort of understanding which is at work in our encounter with and participation in a cultural tradition – something which is prior to any systematic hermeneutic investigation. This process of coming-to-understanding is not a matter of unprejudiced appropriation of an object such as a text, but a 'fusion' of one's own 'horizon' of meanings and expectations ('prejudices') with that of the text, the other person, the alien culture.

Gadamer is therefore not offering a different methodology of understanding; nor is he 'against method' in Feyerabend's sense. Rather, he is concerned with processes which precede and underlie interpretative methods:

The hermeneutics developed here is not, therefore, a methodology of the human sciences, but an attempt to understand what the human sciences truly are, beyond their methodological self-consciousness, and what connects them with the totality of our experience of the world.[14]

Does this mean that Gadamer's hermeneutic philosophy leaves practical hermeneutics as it is? Gadamer tends to argue as if it does, but it is clear that his critique of what he calls objectivism threatens any conception of hermeneutics which expects to grasp, once and for all, determinate meanings in a text. In so doing, it also cuts away the ground from similarly objectivistic conceptions of the social sciences.

It might seem, then, that a realist defence of the social sciences should take its stand on issues of textual interpretation. As we have seen, Gadamer's hermeneutics represents a considerable departure from the tradition of Schleiermacher, Dilthey and their successors; indeed his major work, *Truth and Method*, is designed precisely as a critique of that mainstream tradition and its 'methodological' conception of understanding.[15] One way of upholding a realist conception of the social sciences might then be to revert to a more objectivistic conception of hermeneutics, represented today, in different ways, by such writers as Emilio Betti, E. D. Hirsch, U. Oevermann and H. J. Sandkühler.[16]

To do this, however, would be to miss the force of Gadamer's central notion of the primacy of encounter and engagement – something surely of crucial importance for the social sciences, given that they are so bound up with social and political ideologies. Thus rather than look in detail at the ways in which other writers in the hermeneutic tradition have attempted to defend what they often describe as the objectivity of interpretation, I shall assume for the purposes of argument that Gadamer has given a more or less adequate account of the 'bottom line' of all interpretation and understanding.

What are the implications of this conception for the human and social sciences? One answer can be found in a dense passage from *Truth and Method*:

> Obviously we cannot speak of an object of research in the human sciences in the sense appropriate to the natural sciences, where research penetrates more and more deeply into nature. Rather, in the human sciences the interest in tradition is motivated in a special way by the present and its interests. The theme and area of research are actually constituted by the motivation of the enquiry. Hence historical research is based on the historical movement in which life itself stands and cannot be understood

teleologically in terms of the object into which it is enquiring. Such an object clearly does not exist at all in itself. Precisely this is what distinguishes the human sciences from the natural sciences. Whereas the object of the natural sciences can be described idealiter as what would be known in the perfect knowledge of nature, it is senseless to speak of a perfect knowledge of history, and for this reason is it not possible to speak of an object in itself towards which its research is directed.[17]

There are a number of issues here. First, we need to look more closely at Gadamer's contrast between penetration of nature and a present-oriented 'interest in tradition'. It is difficult to make much sense of this except as describing the poles of a continuum between those sciences or research topics which are concerned with the meticulous investigation of a given area of reality, and those which are more a matter of reinterpreting a partially known reality in terms of current concerns. The latter description might fit, say, environmental science as well as the social sciences.

In making his contrast with the human sciences, Gadamer seems to have drawn an unduly objectivistic picture of the sciences of nature which leaves little room for the universality of hermeneutics. In other words, he seems to be invoking the conception mocked by Rorty that there is some way of describing nature which is 'Nature's own'. But it surely does not make sense to talk even 'idealiter' of a perfect knowledge of nature; as I argued earlier, realism is not committed to any such conception. What it *is* committed to is the notion of things existing independently of our descriptions of them, but this would apply equally to certain objects of historical research. It seems to me simply false to say that no historical event exists 'in itself'. What we need here is a more nuanced form of argument, in which the present-orientation of historical research means that the most interesting questions do indeed concern varied possibilities of interpreting historical events. And this *does* set limits to the 'penetrating' power of the historical and social sciences and shows up the limitations of what Giddens has called the 'oversimple revelatory model of social science'[18] – 'a science of society which would reproduce, in the study of human social life, the same kind of sensational illumination and explanatory power already yielded up by the sciences of nature.'[19]

This is the crux of the issues raised by Gadamer and, in a rather different way, by Habermas: it is clear that hermeneutic problems impinge in a stronger and more direct way on the historical-social sciences. What is not clear is whether this entails anti-naturalistic conclusions, as both Gadamer and Habermas assume. Both writers tend to ground their arguments in terms of the nature of our *interest* in social phenomena. This is the dominant theme in the passage quoted above; it is developed further, as we shall see in the next chapter, in Habermas's differentiation of three cognitive interests: control, communication and emancipation. In Gadamer's case the emphasis is generally on cultural *traditions* as the locus of understanding (*Verständigung*), whereas Habermas tends to refer directly to notions of communication and communicative action.

But reference to interests is, from a realist point of view, only a half-way stage in a possible anti-naturalist argument, since the interest-relativity of alternative descriptions does not conflict with the realist postulate of a reality made up of intransitive objects which exist independently of these descriptions. The essential anti-naturalist argument is one which denies the reality of such objects. Gadamer adopts this position in the passage quoted above, but in a lapidary and unconvincing way, based on an overdrawn contrast between the sciences of nature and history.

This is the point at which Gadamer's general thesis spills over into a set of special theses about the place of hermeneutics in the social sciences. These have been developed less by Gadamer himself than by social theorists, notably Habermas and Giddens, as well as by philosophers like Paul Ricoeur and Charles Taylor. The rest of this chapter will discuss these contributions, though Habermas's critical theory will be treated more systematically in Chapter 5.

Earlier traditions of hermeneutic thinking in the social sciences centred on the concept of meaning. In Max Weber's classic formulation, 'the course of human action and human expressions of every sort are open to an interpretation in terms of meaning [*sinnvolle Deutung*] which in the case of other objects would have an analogy only on the level of metaphysics.'[20] Weber attempted to incorporate this concept of interpretation into his account of social scientific explanation, and thus to bridge the chasm which Dilthey and others had dug between 'explanation' and 'understanding'. This story does not need to be re-told here. What matters in the present context is that, in terms of a broader hermeneutic conception such as Gadamer's, this conception of understanding retains a dichotomy between subject and object and an objectivistic conception of interpretive method. It therefore neglects the element of existential encounter in communication which is prior to any systematic social theory. As Giddens put it in *New Rules of Sociological Method*, '*verstehen* must be regarded, not as a special method of entry to the social world peculiar to the social sciences, but as the ontological condition of human society as it is produced and reproduced by its members.'[21] This Heideggerian insight converges with some major traditions in social theory. First and most generally, the symbolic interactionist approach, with its stress on actors' definitions of the situation. Secondly, Alfred Schutz's insistence, *contra* Weber, that typification is a process carried out by actors within the 'life-world' as well as by social scientists, and that the social scientist's data 'are the already constituted meanings of active participants in the social world.'[22] Thirdly, Wittgenstein's notion, developed by Peter Winch, of language games embedded in forms of life.

These variants of *Verstehende* sociology are often loosely described as hermeneutics, and they certainly seem at first sight to correspond to the requirements of a hermeneutically oriented approach to the social world. They are however vulnerable to a broadly-based hermeneutic critique which argues, in essence, that their conception of meaning is too restricted and that they do not do justice to the hermeneutic basis of social theory.

It is important to distinguish the way in which these traditions understood and represented themselves methodologically from the ultimate implications of their theories. Both the symbolic interactionists and Schutz (at least after his emigration) formed something of a counter-culture to the dominant positivist traditions in the United States, and they inevitably adopted some of the metatheoretical assumptions of that milieu. Blumer remained tied in many ways to a positivistic conception of 'empirical science', as did many later writers in the interactionist tradition.[23] Schutz was an enthusiastic admirer of systematic theory in economics, 'the social science that has achieved the highest degree of unification of its conceptual schemes',[24] and in the work of Talcott Parsons.[25] He therefore vacillated between a strong 'postulate of adequacy'[26] and the much weaker claim that systematic theory should not entirely lose contact with the life-world:

in economics, as in all the other social sciences, we always can – and for certain purposes must – go back to the activity of subjects within the social world: to their ends, motives, choices and preferences.[27]

This is how he presented his work to Parsons, as a bridge between Parsonian theory and the real world; Parsons unfortunately did not feel that there was anything to be bridged. Ethnomethodology also seems to be tugged in two different directions. The first is towards an extreme nominalism and phenomenalism about social structures,[28] often pushed to the limit of a totally relativistic position in which any account is as good as any other. The second is a basically empiricist study of the pragmatics of speech which, whatever its merits within linguistics, no longer has much relevance for social theory.

The latter example shows the familiar association between theory and metatheory: here the direction of the influence seems to be that a metatheoretical scepticism about the postulates of orthodox social theory leads to the reassuring solidity of videotapes and transcripts of conversation. In the case of the other variants of *Verstehende* sociology, it is the theoretical focus which seems to me more significant than the metatheoretical glosses. The more telling hermeneutic objection to these theoretical traditions is not to their self-understanding but to their restricted conception of understanding itself. All these approaches confine themselves largely to the study of the 'subjective meanings' actually or supposedly present in the actors' heads, at the expense of the more general underlying structures of meaning which the hermeneutic tradition considers equally important.

Symbolic interactionism, for example, focuses as its name implies on interaction; structural aspects of social life are reduced in a social psychological manner to socialisation, role-taking and related phenomena.[29] Conversely, in the phenomenological tradition, the focus is on cognitive phenomena, the relation between different typifications, such that the whole enterprise comes to resemble a sociology of knowledge and, in Berger and Luckmann's *Social Construction of Reality*,[30] is explicitly presented as such. The related approach recommended by Wittgenstein and Winch brings out more sharply one of the problems which arise here: a language-game and its associated view of the world is not a cab which one can get in and out of at will. The hermeneutic process, to repeat Gadamer's metaphor, is not the replacement of the interpreter's 'horizon' by that of the object of study, but a dialogical process in which the two horizons are fused together. As Habermas put it in an early work:

> Winch seems to have in mind a linguistic version of Dilthey. From his free-floating position the language analyst can slip into and reproduce the grammar of any language-game, without himself being tied to the dogmatism of his own language-game, which would govern the language analysis as such.[31]

This upshot of the hermeneutic critique of *Verstehende* sociology is that it must broaden its concept of meaning and recognise the interactive or 'dialogical' dimension to the clashes between alternative frameworks of meaning. In other words, hermeneutics criticises the restriction to subjective meaning and to an exclusively subject–object conception of science. As Giddens puts it at the end of *New Rules of Sociological Method*:

> The mediation of paradigms or widely discrepant theoretical schemes in science is a hermeneutic matter like that involved in the contacts between other types of meaning-frames. But sociology, unlike natural science, deals with a pre-interpreted world, where the creation and reproduction of meaning-frames is a very condition of that which it seeks to analyse, namely human social conduct: this is why there is a double hermeneutic in the social sciences . . . the observing social scientist has to be able first to grasp those lay concepts, i.e. penetrate hermeneutically the form of life whose features he wishes to analyse or explain.[32]

This need not of course involve a dialogue in the literal sense; the point is that there is a virtual dialogue in which insiders' and observers' conceptions interact. Even when the interpreter feels constrained to reject the actors' view as totally off beam, it remains relevant that the actors have that view and that the interpreter be able to describe it accurately. Much of the time, of course, social science (like any other science) appears as a critique of common-sense conceptions, but it is important to recognise the way in which common sense is also constitutive of the social reality which the members of society produce and reproduce. This is the basis of Giddens's distinction between 'practical consciousness, as tacit stocks of knowledge which actors draw upon in the constitution of social activity, and . . . "discursive consciousness", involving knowledge which actors are able to express on the level of discourse.'[33]

Here Giddens takes on board, but also modifies, the ethnomethodological principle that members of society should not be treated as 'cultural dopes' but as knowledgeable and skilled performers who 'bring off' society as a practical accomplishment. However, where ethnomethodology conflates practical and discursive consciousness and all too often treats them as invulnerable to sociological critique, Giddens insists on the distinction:

> The logical status of the knowledge applied by social actors in the production and reproduction of social systems . . . has to be considered on two levels. On the methodological level, what I label 'mutual knowledge' is a non-corrigible resource which the social analyst necessarily depends upon, as the medium of generating 'valid' descriptions of social life. As Wittgenstein shows, to know a form of life is to be able in principle to participate in it. But the validity of descriptions or characterisations of social activity is a distinct issue from the validity of 'knowledge' as belief-claims constituted in the discourse of social actors.[34]

So far, I have argued for the acceptance of the hermeneutic approach to social theory and the associated critique of various forms of *Verstehende* sociology. In the rest of this chapter I shall indicate some limitations of the hermeneutic programme and set the scene for a discussion in subsequent chapters of the ways in which social theory can go beyond it. I should stress in advance that I consider these criticisms to be matters of social theory rather than philosophical metatheory; in other words, they are not specifically realist arguments. On the other hand, the criticisms I shall make of existing *Verstehende* sociologies and of hermeneutic metatheory may provide some further support for a naturalist position on social science.

The natural starting-point for this discussion is again the concept of critique. I shall suggest that, while it is wrong to reject hermeneutics as *per se* uncritical, it does have problems in handling what Habermas calls systematically distorted communication, and this points us beyond hermeneutics to more structuralist and materialist conceptions of social theory – themselves of course hermeneutically grounded.

It is easy to see how the impression has arisen that hermeneutic theory is uncritical. In its association with theological apologetics and with aesthetics it has traditionally been concerned to find meaning, truth and beauty even in the most unpromising locations. As Paul Ricoeur put it at the beginning of *Freud and Philosophy*, hermeneutics is polarized between two projects: the 'recollection of meaning' and the 'exercise of suspicion':

> According to the one pole, hermeneutics is understood as the manifestation and restoration of a meaning addressed to me in the manner of a message, a proclamation, or as is sometimes said, a kerygma; according to the other pole, it is understood as a demystification, as a reduction of illusion.[35]

Gadamer's conception of hermeneutics is well towards the former pole: this emerges most starkly in his opposition to Habermas's stress on emancipation:

> the purpose of sociological method as emancipating one from tradition places it at the outset very far from the traditional purpose and starting point of the hermeneutical problematic with all its bridge building and recovery of the best in the past.[36]

Gadamer goes on to reject the critique of authority which Habermas takes over from the Enlightenment;[37] he concludes severely:

> The unavoidable consequence to which all these observations lead is that the basically emancipatory consciousness must have in mind the dissolution of all authority, all obedience. This means that unconsciously the ultimate guiding image of emancipatory reflection in the social sciences must be an anarchistic utopia. Such an image, however, seems to me to reflect a hermeneutically false consciousness.[38]

Passages like these, however, say more about Gadamer's personal conservatism than about the intrinsic nature of his hermeneutic philosophy. As Ricoeur has shown in his discussion of the exchanges between Gadamer and Habermas, the latter's critique of ideologies, though distinct from hermeneutic reflection – not to be conflated with it – is not radically incompatible with it.[39] Habermas's positive programme, the latest form of which is presciently recommended in Ricoeur's article, will be discussed in detail in the next chapter. Here I shall confine myself to showing its origins, or at least one of its important sources, in his critique of the universality of hermeneutics. As Habermas puts it, 'Hermeneutic consciousness remains incomplete as long as it does not include a reflection upon the limits of hermeneutic understanding.'[40] Habermas summarises

> four aspects in which a philosophical hermeneutic is relevant to the sciences and the interpretation of their results. (1) Hermeneutic consciousness destroys the objectivist self-understanding of the traditional *Geisteswissenschaften*. It follows from the hermeneutic situatedness of the interpreting scientist that objectivity in understanding cannot be secured by an abstraction from preconceived ideas, but only by reflecting upon the context of effective-history which connects perceiving subjects and their object. (2) Hermeneutic consciousness furthermore reminds the social sciences of problems which arise from the symbolic pre-structuring of their object. If the access to data is no longer mediated through controlled observation but through communication in everyday language, then theoretical concepts can no longer be operationalised within the framework of the pre-scientifically developed language-game of physical measuring . . . (3) Hermeneutic consciousness also affects the scientistic self-understanding of the natural sciences . . . The legitimation of decisions which direct the choice of research strategies, the construction of theories and the methods for testing them, and which thereby determine the 'progress of science', is dependent on discussions within the community of scientists . . . A philosophical hermeneutic can show the reason why it is possible to arrive at a rationally motivated but not at a peremptory consensus on this theoretic level. (4) Hermeneutic consciousness is, finally, called upon in . . . the translation of

important scientific information into the language of the social life-world.[41]

What then is Habermas' argument for the 'limits of hermeneutic understanding'? He has essentially two related objections: firstly a general objection to its 'linguistic idealism' (*Idealismus der Sprachlichkeit*);[42] secondly, a more specific claim that hermeneutics cannot deal with 'systematically distorted communication'. The general criticism is outlined in Habermas's discussion of Gadamer in *Zur Logik der Sozialwissenschaften*. It is not enough to consider, as Gadamer does, a context of tradition made up of symbolic meaning:

> It makes good sense to construe language as a kind of meta-institution on which all social institutions depend, since social action is constituted only in communication in ordinary language. But this meta-institution of language as tradition is clearly itself dependent on social processes which are not just normative relations. Language is *also* a medium of domination and social power . . . [and, he adds, work] . . . Hermeneutic experience, when it comes up against this dependence of symbolic structures on real (*faktisch*) circumstances, turns into the critique of ideology.[43]

Gadamer rejects this argument, repeating his slogan that 'being that can be understood is language':

> This does not mean that there is a world of meanings that is narrowed down to the status of secondary objects of knowledge and mere supplements to the economic and political realities that fundamentally determine the life of society. Rather it means that the mirror of language reflects everything that is.[44]

This looks like one of those clashes between two paradigms in which neither will give way to the other. Habermas therefore concentrates, in his 'Universality' essay, on a more specific argument which he had adumbrated in *Zur Logik der Sozialwissenschaften*.[45] The term 'systematically distorted communication' refers to the manipulations which psychoanalysis aims to decode: dream-actions, rationalised parapraxes, displacement activities and so on. In psychoanalysis,

> These manifestations can be regarded as parts of systematically distorted communication. They are comprehensible only to the extent to which the general conditions of the pathology of everyday communication are known. A theory of everyday communication would therefore have to beat a path through to the pathologically blocked meaning-context.[46]

In other words, as he put it in *Zur Logik der Sozialwissenschaften*:

> The language analysis which deciphers repressed interpretations as unconscious motives goes beyond the dimension of subjectively intended meaning and of cultural tradition.[47]

These considerations are relevant in two ways. First, this kind of pseudo-communication may not be confined to individual psychopathology, but may exist, as ideological distortion, in social systems as well – in which case it would require a similarly systematic and more-than-hermeneutic analysis.[48] Second, the mere fact that this type of understanding exists shows that we need something more than hermeneutics to explain its possibility: we need a *'theory of communicative competence'*.[49]

As we shall see in the next chapter, Habermas devoted much of his attention in the 1960s to working out these analogies between psychoanalysis and the critique of ideology and their status as critical sciences governed by an emancipatory interest and using a mixture of understanding and causal analysis. In the past decade, his emphasis has shifted towards the second theme, the development of a theory of communicative competence, which has gradually broadened into a more general theory of communicative action. Here he has returned to, and built on, his general critique of hermeneutic idealism. This is, it seems to me, the more fundamental. The problem for hermeneutic theory is not just that communication may be systematically distorted by extraneous causal influences,[50] but that linguistic communication is anyway part of more general social processes, which should not be reduced to communication alone. The thesis of hermeneutic universality commits, once again, the epistemic fallacy: from the fact that interpretative processes are a significant part of what goes on in the social world, and that our access to the social world is necessarily via our understanding of these interpretative processes (Giddens's double hermeneutic), it does not follow that this is all that exists, or can be known to exist. The production and reproduction of social structures is partly a matter of the interpretations given to them by actors, but also of what Durkheim called 'deeper causes which are opaque to consciousness'.

5

Realism and Critical Theory

The 'critical theory' of what came to be called the Frankfurt School has been so fully discussed that there is no point in providing yet another outline history here.[1] I shall be concerned almost entirely with the work of Jürgen Habermas, and I shall refer to the earlier generation of critical theorists only to set the scene for a juxtaposition of Habermas and Bhaskar.

At the end of the preceding chapter I presented and endorsed Habermas's methodological demand that hermeneutics be supplemented by some sort of systematic critical procedure. This is not only a persistent theme in Habermas's work; it is also an expression of the defining characteristic of critical theory: its orientation to emancipation. The critical theorists took up Marx's early conception of a unity between philosophy and the proletariat in their own programme for interdisciplinary Marxist social science. As Max Horkheimer put it in two early essays:

> [Critical theory] . . . is not just a research hypothesis which shows its value in the ongoing business of men; it is an essential element in the historical effort to create a world which satisfies the needs and powers of men. However extensive the interaction between the critical theory and the special sciences whose progress the theory must respect and on which it has for decades exercised a liberating and stimulating influence, the theory never aims simply at an increase of knowledge as such. Its goal is man's emancipation from slavery.[2]

> What decides the value of a theory is not only the formal criterion of truth, [but more] its connection with the tasks which are

undertaken by progressive social forces at a particular historical moment.[3]

As is well known, the critical theorists became increasingly pessimistic about the efficacy and even the existence of these 'progressive social forces'. What is not so often noted is the concommitant process of their withdrawal, towards the end of their period of exile in the USA, from social science into philosophy. Horkheimer and Adorno had come to see the social sciences not just as 'uncritical' but as the embodiment of instrumental reason, the cutting edge of 'the indefatigable self-destructiveness of enlightenment'.[4] As Habermas notes,[5] this makes one wonder why they re-established an Institute of *Social* Research, but it also helps to explain the passion behind Adorno's critique of empirical social research and the rest of the 'Positivist dispute'.[6]

Habermas, by contrast, has always cast his version of critical theory in terms of a metacritique of the social sciences, rather than a return to the philosophy of consciousness. 'A radical critique of knowledge', he announced in the preface to *Knowledge and Human Interests*, 'is possible only as social theory.'[7] Moreover, his critique of positivism in the sciences has always been fuelled by his opposition to technocratic forms of social engineering and political manipulation. This can be seen in his first book, *Strukturwandel der Öffentlichkeit* (1962), where the decline of the public sphere is reflected in a 'social-psychological dissolution' of the concept of public opinion: this ceases to be a critical instance in which the public passes judgement on affairs of state, and becomes instead a mere quantity of approval/disapproval, to be measured and manipulated.[8] The titles of Habermas's writings in the 1960s testify to this constant preoccupation: 'Technology and Science as Ideology', 'Theory and Practice in a Scientised Civilisation', 'The Scientisation of Politics and Public Opinion', 'Theory of Society or Social Technology?'.

This chapter is essentially concerned with the question whether Habermas's critique of positivism in the social sciences entails an anti-naturalist position. And behind this question in the philosophy of science there is a further question in general philosophy: whether a transcendentalist position of the kind which Habermas has seemed to accept is necessarily opposed to realism, as Norman Stockman believes, or compatible with it, as Deryck Beyleveld suggests. The first question, then, is about realist naturalism; the second about realism *tout court*. It makes sense therefore to deal with the latter question first.

In *Knowledge and Human Interests*, Habermas presented the metatheory of the sciences which he had sketched out in his Frankfurt inaugural lecture of 1965.[9] The book was, he wrote, 'a historically oriented attempt to reconstruct the prehistory of modern positivism with the systematic intention of analyzing the connections between knowledge and interest.'[10] Historically oriented, because positivist philosophy on the one hand, and the transition from Kant to Hegel and Marx on the other, had suppressed the theory of knowledge, leaving only the philosophy of science or methodology. The consequence is what Habermas, following Husserl, calls 'objectivism':

> Once epistemology has been flattened out to methodology, it loses sight of the constitution of the objects of possible experience; in the same way, a formal science dissociated from transcendental reflection becomes blind to the genesis of rules for the combination of symbols. In Kantian terms, both ignore the synthetic achievements of the knowing subject . . . . Objectivism deludes the sciences with the image of a self-subsistent world of facts structured in a lawlike manner; it thus conceals the *a priori* constitution of these facts. It can no longer be effectively overcome from without, from the position of a repurified epistemology, but only by a methodology that transcends its own boundaries.[11]

Habermas identifies positivism with the denial or renunciation of this process of reflection.[12] And in this sense realism too appears as a variety of positivism. As Stockman puts it:

> The problem with metaphysical realism, from the standpoint of critical theory, is that it is a pre-critical philosophical position, since it attempts to conceptualise an independent reality without raising the question of the constitution of that 'reality' through synthetic activity.[13]

Or in other words, in neither scientific realism nor critical rationalism is the argument recognised, that to ascribe 'independent reality' to an object of knowledge is not (to use Kant's expressions) to enlarge the concept of that object but 'to express the relation of the concept to the faculty of knowledge'.[14]

Stockman is right that, from the point of a transcendentalist epistemology, realism cannot be more than a dogma, or at best a regulative principle for a *methodology* of science. Although it is not meaningless, as it was in the strongest formulations of logical positivism, we may only believe it to be true; we cannot know it to be true. To believe that we can is to commit what Beyleveld calls the 'ontic fallacy', the reduction of knowledge of being to being. Although Habermas himself has had very little to say about realism, he accepts the anti-realist conclusion that

· *any* transcendental approach, in the last analysis, precludes that there can be any such thing as truthfulness to reality in the sense postulated by scientific realism.[15]

The issues at stake here seem once again to be those discussed in Chapter 2 in relation to Beyleveld's position. In fact, however, it is not at all clear that these *are* the relevant issues for Habermas, since he has never adopted a pure transcendentalist approach and has been increasingly concerned to distance himself from the 'fundamentalistic' programme of transcendental philosophy. In the preface to *Theory of Communicative Action*, and again in the final section of the book, he makes this very clear. Critical theory, he reminds us, has always been dubious about the 'systematic' claims of philosophy, and he endorses, citing Rorty in a footnote, the pragmatist and hermeneutic objections to 'any kind of fundamentalism'.[16] And he now concedes that 'the attempt [in *Knowledge and Human Interests*] to ground critical social theory by way of the *theory of knowledge*, while it did not lead astray, was indeed a roundabout way.'[17]

What did Habermas try to do in *Knowledge and Human Interests*? In turning to look at this book in more detail, we shall see the interconnections between his 'quasi-transcendental' approach and his anti-naturalist arguments. In the passage quoted above from *Knowledge and Human Interest*,[18] Habermas claimed that objectivism 'can no longer be effectively overcome from without, from the position of a repurified epistemology, but only by a methodology that transcends its own boundaries'.

This 'methodology' involves a distinction between three types of science, each grounded in a specific knowledge-guiding interest:

1. '[T]heories of the empirical sciences disclose reality subject to the constitutive interest in the possible securing and expansion, through information, of feedback-monitored action. This is the cognitive interest in technical control over objectified processes.'

2. '[H]ermeneutic inquiry discloses reality subject to a constitutive interest in the preservation and expansion of the intersubjectivity of possible action-oriented mutual understanding.'

3. 'Critical' social sciences, notably psychoanalysis and the critique of ideology, are governed, like philosophy, by an emancipatory cognitive interest which operates through self-reflection (and thus distinguishes between 'invariant regularities of social action' as such and 'ideologically frozen relations of dependence that can in principle be transformed.'[19]

Habermas uses the term 'constitutive' in the technical sense of neo-Kantian philosophy. The interest in technical control is what makes empirical reality meaningful to the observer, and determines what is to count as an object of knowledge or an empirical statement about such an object.

In the behavioural system of instrumental action, reality is constituted as the totality of what can be experienced from the viewpoint of possible technical control. The reality that is objectified under these transcendental conditions has its counterpart in a specifically restricted mode of experience. The language of empirical-analytic statements about reality is formed under the same conditions.[20]

This is the sense in which the cognitive interests, and in particular the technical interest,[21] are transcendental in their functioning. At the same time, however, they generate 'methodological rules for the organisation of processes of inquiry' rather than principles of 'pure theoretical reason'. More generally, they arise from actual structures of human life: from structures of a species that reproduces its life both through learning processes of socially organised labour and processes of mutual understanding in interactions mediated in ordinary language.[22]

Habermas never really clarified the ambiguities in this model, of which perhaps the most important is its status. How strictly should we take the language of transcendental constitution? Are the cognitive interests to be understood as governing radically distinct types of science, or as ideal-typical poles to which actual sciences or specialisms might correspond more or less closely?[23]

There are three interrelated issues here: (1) the transcendentalist formulation of the cognitive interest model, (2) its methodological dualism or anti-naturalism and (3) within this dualism, Habermas's characterisation of the technical interest. Let us look first at the prima facie anti-realist implications of (1) and (3).

It does seem that Habermas's notion of the technical interest in prediction and control which governs empirical science derives some of its plausibility from certain classical formulations in positivist and early pragmatist philosophies of science: in particular Comte and C. S. Peirce. Habermas's claim, in essence, is that Peirce explains this fundamental principle of empirical science which was not adequately grasped by positivists like Comte and Mach.[24] As a result, Habermas does not argue as fully as he might for this instrumentally oriented conception of natural science and technocratic social science. From the standpoint of a realist philosophy of science, this instrumental conception would need to be defended in more sociological terms as something more like an empirical thesis about the pragmatics of research Thomas McCarthy puts the issue very well:

The question is . . . . What do [the statements of empirical science], if valid, disclose about reality? Does their meaning bear an intrinsic relation to possibilities of action of a certain sort?

Habermas' response – that empirical–analytic inquiry provides information that is technically utilisable – would be widely agreed to, if somewhat less interesting, were it intended in a realist sense. If science could be conceived as presenting or approximating a true picture of the regular order of a nature-in-itself, it would follow routinely that this information might be put to practical use. The thesis of the technical interest guiding science has a bite only if understood in a quasi-transcendental sense: as making a claim about the conditions of possibility of objectively valid knowledge of nature and thus about the very meaning of scientific statements.[25]

Even on this strong formulation, however, it is not clear that there is a conflict here with Bhaskar's transcendental realism, given his principle of epistemological relativism:

whenever we speak of things or of events etc. in science we must always speak of them and know them under particular descriptions, descriptions which will always be to a greater or lesser extent theoretically determined, which are not neutral reflections of a given world.[26]

It follows that, *if* Habermas is right about the technical interest, our descriptions will be ('quasi-transcendentally') loaded in the way he describes. There seems no reason why the realist cannot accept as a hypothesis this input from specific and differential cognitive interests, while continuing to insist on the existence of a domain of intransitive objects as itself a transcendental (and not merely quasi-transcendental) ground of scientific practice. At this point, however, Habermas's notion of the quasi-transcendental status of the cognitive interests reveal itself as not just a vague formulation but the locus of a paradox:

in attempting to combine a 'transcendental' with a 'naturalistic' approach to the subjective conditions of knowledge, Habermas appears to be caught in a dilemma: either nature has the transcendental status of a constituted objectivity and cannot, therefore, be the ground of the constituting subject; or nature is the ground of subjectivity and cannot, therefore, be simply a constituted objectivity.[27]

McCarthy goes on to discuss Habermas's attempts to resolve this dilemma, concluding that it 'does not seem to have been resolved'.[28] Habermas himself has become more and more doubtful about the status of the cognitive interest model and his 'quasi-transcendental' formulation of it in 1968. What remains in his emergent theory of communicative action is a much less transcendentalist and more pragmatic distinction between two forms of experience and action. With this reformulation, as we shall see, Habermas distances himself further from the foundationalist claims of traditional philosophy, while making strong realist claims for reconstructive sciences such as the theory of communicative action. For the purposes of my argument here, the important point is that, while his model remains strongly dualistic, the synthesis which was constructed in epistemological terms in 1968, under the name critical science, now appears in social scientific terms as a fusion of system and life-world perspectives, those of the external observer and those of the participant.

It is worth tracing this development of Habermas's thought in some detail. First, he gives a more modest gloss to the claims advanced in *Knowledge and Human Interests*:

> My interpretation of Peirce and Dilthey has I think yielded enough indications for the conjecture that the use of categories like 'bodies in motion' or 'acting and speaking individuals' implies an *a priori* relation to action to the extent that 'observable bodies' are simultaneously 'instrumentally manipulable' whereas 'understandable persons' are simultaneously 'participants in linguistically mediated interaction'.[29]

There are, I think, two shifts of emphasis here: a scaling-down of the epistemological claims and a shift from epistemological issues to a focus on action. These are reinforced by a second major qualification: a sharper distinction between what in another tradition would be called the context of discovery and the context of justification:

> In the investigations up to this point I have brought out the interrelation between knowledge and interest, without making clear the critical threshold between communication (which remains embedded within the context of action) and discourses (which transcend the compulsions of action). To be sure, the constitution of scientific object domains can be conceived as a continuation of the objectivations which we undertake in the world of social life prior to all science. But the genuine claim to objectivity which is raised with the instauration of science is based

on a virtualisation of the pressure of experience and decision, and
it is only this which permits a discursive testing of *hypothetical*
claims to validity and thus the generation of *rationally grounded
knowledge.*[30]

Habermas retains the concept of constitution, but now stresses
that 'the construction of a world of objects of possible experience'
involves 'a systematic interplay of sensuous reception, action and
linguistic representation':[31]

With regard to the constitution of the world of experience, we
distinguish between two object-domains (things, events; persons,
expressions), to which correspond different modes of experience
(sensory, communicative), two different forms of empirical
language (physical and intentional language), and two types of
action (instrumental, communicative).[32]

The concept of communicative action, distinguished from
instrumental action in *Knowledge and Human Interests* as the
context of differential object-constitution, increasingly comes into
its own as 'a basic concept of sociology',[33] moving towards its
apotheosis in the two massive volumes of *The Theory of
Communicative Action.* This marks his turn away from
transcendental language towards a theory of communicative action,
and establishes the logical status of that theory as a rational
reconstruction of universal human competences.[34]

Habermas claimed in 1968 that critical social science operates in
terms of self-reflection, which 'releases the subject from
dependence on hypostatized powers'.[35] After completing
Knowledge and Human Interests, he realised

that the traditional use of the term 'reflection' which goes back to
German idealism, covers (and confuses) two things: on the one
hand, it denotes the reflection upon the conditions of potential
abilities of a knowing, speaking and acting subject as such; on the
other hand, it denotes the reflection upon unconsciously
produced constraints to which a determinate subject (or a
determinate group of subjects, or a determinate species-subject)
succumbs in its process of self-reflection.[36]

The first of these processes is what Habermas now calls rational reconstruction, where what is reconstructed is the pretheoretical knowledge (knowing how, in Ryle's sense) of actors. The paradigm case is Chomsky's theory of linguistic competence, which Habermas has broadened into a theory of communicative competence.[37] Theories of this kind correspond roughly to what Habermas had earlier called depth hermeneutics, which does not merely clarify obscure expressions but elucidates the systematic principles which produce them. This means that a reconstructive science does not simply replace a prescientific description, as in the natural sciences;[38] on the contrary, the test of its validity is its compatibility with the tacit knowledge of, for example, native speakers of a language.

This conception, in which a structure of, for example, syntactic rules produces observable phenomena, should be immediately recognisable as a realist form of explanation. Habermas makes this explicit, saying that whereas theoretical descriptions in empirical science *may* be given a realist interpretation, reconstructions *must* be.

> Of course, one can say that theoretical descriptions correspond (if true) to certain structures of reality in the same sense as reconstructions bear a likeness (if correct) to the deep structures explicated. On the other hand, the asserted correspondence between a descriptive theory and an object allows of many epistemological interpretations other than the realistic (e.g. instrumentalist or conventionalist). Rational reconstructions, on the contrary, can reproduce the pretheoretical knowledge that they explicate only in an essentialist sense; if they are true, they have to correspond precisely to the rules that are operatively effective in the object domain – that is, to the rules that actually determine the production of surface structures.[39]

In making this argument, Habermas draws explicitly on Chomsky's claims about speakers' implicit knowledge of grammatical rules. These claims are open to quite serious objections such as those made by Quine. Even if Quine has his own problems in restricting himself to notions of stimulus meaning, he may well be right about the difficulties in giving much empirical meaning to Chomsky's claims. As Quine puts it:

According to this doctrine, two extensionally equivalent systems of grammatical rules need not be equally correct. The right rules are the rules that the native speakers somehow have implicitly in mind. It is the grammarian's task to find the right rules, in this sense . . . . [Thus the 'new doctrine'] . . . imputes to the natives an unconscious preference for one system of rules over another, equally unconscious, which is extensionally equivalent to it.[40]

But as we saw in Chapters 1 and 2, the fact that a realist interpretation may be difficult to specify in particular areas of science (microphysics being the most favoured source of examples), does not destroy its general plausibility. Habermas is anyway concerned to make a general claim about reconstructions, which gives a dramatically realist twist to the whole of his recent theorising.

What he does, implicitly, is to invert the standard argument of realist anti-naturalists that realism is appropriate to the realm of nature but not to the social world. For Habermas, a realist interpretation of theory is one option among others for the natural sciences and for social sciences which also aim to formulate general laws of objectified processes (e.g. system theories). For reconstructive social theory, by contrast, realism is obligatory.

I shall not discuss in detail the way in which Habermas develops his reconstructive theory of communicative action. Very briefly, he argues that societies must be studied both as life-worlds (as they appear to their members) and as systems of actions integrated in functional terms (as they appear to the observer).[41] For Habermas, even a fully described life-world is not enough for the description of a society:

A 'Verstehende' sociology which reduces society to the life-world, restricts its perspective to the self-interpretation of the culture under investigation; this internal perspective filters out everything which influences a sociocultural life-world from the outside.[42]

When we conceive a society in this way as a life-world, we take on board three fictions: we assume (a) the autonomy of the actors, (b) the independence of culture and (c) the transparency of communication.[43]

On the other hand, a system perspective is similarly incomplete on its own: 'The entities which, in the external perspective of the observer, are to be subsumed under system-theoretical concepts, must *first* be identified as the life-worlds of social groups and understood in their symbolic structures.'[44]

Now whatever the substantive merits of this programme, which is still in a very preliminary stage,[45] it is clear that it puts in a very different light the standard conception of Habermasian theory as ultimately transcendentalist and anti-realist. What of the anti-naturalist implications of the original programme? It is clear that Habermas now recognises that the triadic cognitive interest model was much too crude. More importantly, it was too 'cognitive' and insufficiently sociological. As we noted above, the focus has now shifted to the contrast between instrumental and communicative action, which were previously analysed more as reference-points (*Handlungsbezüge*) of two types of *cognition*. In other words, his earlier attempt to socialise or sociologise epistemology did not go far enough. In the present model, it seems that instrumental and strategic action are coordinated with social scientific perspectives such as system theory, and communicative action with those oriented to the life-world – the perspectives of observer and participant, respectively. (Perhaps one should say virtual participant, since a social scientist operating within the perspective of the life-world need not (and in many cases, of course, cannot) *directly* participate in the life-world under investigation.)

Even here, no doubt, the distinctions are drawn too sharply, as one can see in Habermas's insensitivity to the possibility of game-theoretic reconstructions ('strategic action', for Habermas) of prima facie communicative action. Be that as it may, there no longer seems to be a sharp antithesis between 'technical-instrumental and practical-communicative' knowledge as Habermas had argued in *Knowledge and Human Interests* with reference to Peirce and Dilthey.

It may be helpful here to refer again to Norman Stockman's Habermasian critique of realist naturalism. Stockman concedes that Habermas's construction of one pole of the antithesis, the technical-instrumental orientation of empirical science, was overly influenced by positivist conceptions of natural science.

So long as scientific realism is not taken in its essentialist, objectivist form to be specifying the essence of science as such, but rather, as has been suggested here, is interpreted as a descriptive methodology appropriate to a particular phase in the development of certain natural sciences, the realist theory provides evidence of precisely that which Habermas denies, namely the possibility of the emergence of alternative methodological categories under which knowledge in the natural sciences can be organised.[46]

But critical theory must remain radically anti-naturalistic, for two essential reasons: the form of experience in which social situations are given to us, and, relatedly, the criteria by which we form concepts of those situations.

Structures of social relationships are not 'unobservable' in the same sense as elementary particles or black holes; it is not that they are inaccessible to human sensory experience, requiring instead sociological equivalents of bubble chambers and radio telescopes in order to be perceived, but rather that they are only accessible to a form of experience which goes beyond sensory experience, namely communicative experience.[47]

Realists wrongly assume

that the theoretical concepts of the social sciences refer to 'theoretical entities' in the same way as those of the natural sciences. But the reflexivity of ordinary language, to which the concepts of the social sciences are indissolubly bound, precludes the formulation of unambiguous demonstrative and recognitive criteria for the referents of theoretical concepts, whose selection and significance remain hermeneutically linked to 'an anticipatory interpretation of society as a whole'.[48]

There is a good deal to be said for this position, and I shall return to it in the next chapter, but it is not clear that it is any longer Habermas's view. He retains the orientation to ordinary language and to communicative action within 'the context-creating horizon of the life-world',[49] but he now wants to make *stronger* claims, if anything, about what goes on there than he thinks can be made about nature.

This is not to say that Habermas would feel comfortable with a realist naturalism of the kind developed by Bhaskar. He ends a recent conference paper with a ringing critique of

the one-sided orientation of Western philosophy to the world of being. To the primacy of *ontological* thinking correspond the privileging of cognition in epistemology and philosophy of science and the methodical singling-out of assertory sentences in semantics. The formal-pragmatic investigation of mutual understanding as a whole can dissolve these fixations. Against this ontological and cognitivistic one-sidedness it can bring to fruition a decentred understanding of the world which begins by linking together the objective world with the social and the subjective world and demands a simultaneous orientation to the corresponding validity-claims of propositional truth, normative rightness, and sincerity or authenticity.[50]

There are echoes here of Rorty (whom Habermas cites just before the lines quoted above), but the rationalism of the closing phrases goes well beyond anything Rorty would consider possible or desirable. As for realism, Habermas might object to the project and to the 'cognitivist' form of argumentation, but it is not clear what any substantive disagreement would be about.

In case this conclusion sounds too hasty, let me briefly consider three important areas of potential disagreement: correspondence theories of truth, hermeneutics and the fact–value distinction. Habermas is certainly committed to rejecting any realist position which retains a correspondence theory of truth. This theory 'attempts in vain to break out of the linguistic realm in which alone the validity claims of speech acts can be clarified.'[51] Here however there is no apparent disagreement with Bhaskar's position, which also rejects correspondence truth (cf. Chapter 2, above). Secondly, he would undoubtedly want to reject a realist naturalism which neglected hermeneutic issues of the kind discussed in the previous chapter. Again, it does not seem to me that this charge can be raised against Bhaskar's version of naturalism. Finally, it is clear from the remarks about philosophy quoted aove, and from the whole of his previous work, that Habermas would reject any realism which upheld the fact–value distinction in its traditional form. Here again, however, there is an important area of convergence with realism around the theme of emancipatory critique. Roy Bhaskar has argued, in two important articles,[52] that all science has a critical dimension and that, in the domain of the social sciences, this critique has an emancipatory potential. Bhaskar's claim, in a nutshell, is that the scientific critique of a false belief about a social object will tend to include an explanatory critique of the origins and persistence of that false belief. Together these entail, *ceteris paribus*, a condemnation of the causes of the false belief and hence the desirability of showing how those causes might be removed.

This abstract model shares an important feature with Habermas's concept of emancipation grounded in his theory of communicative action: they both enable us to sustain a conception of emancipation which does not rely on a no longer tenable philosophy of history. It may be that this notion of emancipation would seem too 'cognitivist' and generally impoverished to Habermas. This certainly seems to be Stockman's reaction,[53] and it may be that Bhaskar's theory needs to be developed further to bring out the potential changeability of apparently enduring social structures – something for which the notion of dialectical contradiction has been the traditional instrument, from classical Marxism through Adorno and Marcuse and, in a more muted form, Habermas himself.[54]

Be that as it may, the examination of the recent development of Habermas's thought suggests that it is no longer right to see his version of critical theory as in fundamental opposition to a realist naturalism of the kind argued for in this book.

6

Critical Hermeneutics, Realism and the Sociological Tradition

In Chapter 3, I sketched out very briefly the way in which I think realism should deal with the interrelated issues of interpretation, common sense, consensus (in the sense of progress in science) etc. In Chapters 4 and 5, I worked through these claims in more detail, presenting the main themes of hermeneutics and critical theory and trying to show that they can, after all, be incorporated within the realist naturalist position advanced in Chapter 1.

Before turning in the final chapter to more substantive issues in the analysis of action and structure, I should like to bring together the argument of the three preceding chapters in terms of (1) the challenge which hermeneutics and critical theory offer to realism and vice versa; (2) the possibility of a synthesis and (3) the implications of such a synthesis for our understanding of earlier forms of social theory.

As we saw in Chapter 1, hermeneutics, critical theory and realism converged in the critique of positivistic metatheories of social science. Each could claim with some plausibility that its critique went further and deeper than the others. Hermeneutics, in its Gadamerian form, had a built-in claim to universality; critical theory, from its very name, could claim a monopoly of critique, while realism could claim that it tackled the positivist dragon in its lair, on its own terms, and refuted it as a general philosophy of science. From a realist point of view, hermeneutics and critical theory were too equivocal on the latter issue: they side-stepped it in a general critique of objectivism or methodologism, which left positivism, in an admittedly restricted form, unscathed.

Conversely, for hermeneutics and critical theory, realism appeared as just another objectivistic methodology of science.

The demise of positivist philosophy of science, or more precisely its mutation into conventionalism, provided some satisfaction for all three critiques. It showed that all science, and not just social science, was pervaded by an uneasy succession of traditions, between which there raged a conflict of interpretations, and that critique (in admittedly a more limited sense than that asserted by critical theory) was central to the scientific enterprise. Here realism came into its own in offering a transcendentally guaranteed philosophical ontology linked to a sociology of scientific practice.

Three side-issues were eliminated. First, the notion of hermeneutics as a theory restricted to the human sciences was replaced by Gadamer's universalistic conception, while at the same time sociologists largely took on board the notion of a hermeneutic grounding of social theory – Giddens's double hermeneutic. Secondly, Habermas abandoned his 'quasi-transcendental' grounding of science, with its attendant critique of 'mere' methodologies of science, and his epistemological differentiation between types of science in favour of a more pragmatic distinction with less radically anti-naturalist implications. And while he has not embraced a realist position, he has been willing to make extremely strong claims of a realist kind precisely in the domain of the human sciences. Thirdly, the notion of a unique 'critical theory' has been subverted by the realist notion of an emancipatory critique arising directly out of the practice of science.

Thus the horizons of the three critiques have shifted, even if they have not entirely 'fused'. Most crucially, the issue of naturalism has been put in its proper place: that is to say, as an issue to be addressed at the level of social theory and of scientific rather than philosophical ontology. In other words (and I am of course oversimplifying here), the global issue of how far the social sciences resemble the natural sciences has tended to be unpacked into more concrete questions about the nature and status of the entities and mechanisms postulated by theories of social life – the sort of issues addressed in the final chapter of this book.

It would be premature, to say the least, to speak of an emergent synthesis of the three positions discussed here, but my feeling is that what we have are not mutually incommensurable metatheoretical paradigms but differences of emphasis, and theoretical as opposed to metatheoretical disagreements, set against the background of a widely shared conception of the nature and tasks of social theory – a conception which is both substantially different from, and grounded in a more sophisticated way than the earlier positivist consensus.

It *is* undoubtedly premature to make this claim, and it should be taken with a heavy pinch of salt. One could certainly make out a good case for the contrary view that social theory is dissolving into separate and incommensurable research programmes and that the real reason why metatheoretical disputes are disappearing from sight is that they have been swept under the carpet, whence they will reappear in a future period of spring-cleaning such as we had in the 1960s and 1970s. To address this issue seriously would involve an exercise in the sociology of sociology which would be outside the scope of this book. For better or worse, the remaining pages are based on the assumption that we have witnessed the emergence of a degree of consensus within social theory, and that it is compatible with, and supported by, a realist theory of science and a qualified naturalist conception of the social sciences.

In the rest of this chapter I shall follow Parsons's model in *The Structure of Social Action* in evaluating the sociological tradition from the point of view developed above. Like Parsons (who, it will be recalled, devoted only a few pages of that book to Marx), I shall be highly selective in my discussion; unlike him, I shall also be extremely brief, since my *Concept Formation in Social Science* provides a more detailed treatment of these issues. I shall concentrate here on Marx, Durkheim, Max Weber and Parsons himself. I should emphasise that this discussion of the 'founding fathers' is not meant to be ritualistic, since I believe that these writers continue to represent crucially important theoretical options within sociology.

Before looking at the differences between these writers, it is important to recognise what they have in common. All science is basically a matter of reconceptualisation of empirical reality, where this reconceptualisation involves the elucidation of what needs to be the case for empirical reality to appear as it does. What needs to be the case for objects to fall to the ground, for suicide rates to display the systematic regularities and variations which they do, for labour to be expressed in value, for the capitalist economic ethic to emerge in early modern Europe? In the case of the social sciences, there is the further refinement that the specification of their *explananda*, prior to any would-be scientific redescription, must include an account of the 'everyday' conceptualisations of social agents. Even Durkheim, who was notoriously suspicious of the common-sense accounts of social actors, could not define suicide without referring to the actor's knowledge (expectation?) that the act would result in his or her death.

With this important qualification, then, the natural and the social sciences share a common logic, which is basically as described by transcendental realism. This form of scientific practice, however, may be accompanied by a variety of metatheories, more or less adequate to the practice which they aim to describe. In the case of the writers discussed in this chapter, I shall suggest that Marx's largely implicit metatheory is basically a realist one; that of Weber is better described as conventionalist, while Durkheim's position is somewhere in between.

It is notoriously difficult to pin down Marx's philosophical and metatheoretical beliefs. What is most distinctive, however, about Marx and the tradition which he founded is probably the peculiarly intimate dialectical relationship which he postulates between the methods and concepts of science and the objects of inquiry. This is best illustrated by the notion of critique or criticism, which runs right through Marx's work from the 'Critique of Hegel's Philosophy of Right' to *Capital*, the critique of political economy.

Whatever the differences in style, method and subject matter between these two works, they share the underlying theme that the critique of social reality essentially (though by no means exclusively) involves the parallel critique of its theoretical representation, whether this be Hegel's theory of the state or classical political economy. As Marx wrote in the 'Grundrisse':

In the succession of economic categories, as in any other historical, social science, it must not be forgotten that the subject, – here, modern bourgeois society – is always what is given, in the head as well as in reality, and that these categories therefore express the forms of being, the characteristics of existence, and often only individual sides of this specific society, this subject.

The exact development of the concept of capital is necessary . . . just as capital itself, whose abstract, reflected image is its concept, is the foundation of bourgeois society. The sharp formulation of the basic presuppositions of this relation must being out all the contradictions of bourgeois production, as well as the boundary where it drives beyond itself.[1]

There is thus an important sense in which Marx's explanandum in *Capital* is a conceptual question (though one whose answer required detailed empirical as well as conceptual investigations): 'why labour is expressed in value and why the measurement of its duration is expressed in the magnitude of the product.'[2]

Taken together with his materialism, this strongly suggests that Marx is committed to some sort of realist philosophy of science which treats theoretical statements as being about real objects, structures and processes in the world, since in the absence of some such relation between theory and reality it is difficult to see how these 'critiques' could have the explanatory power which Marx ascribes to them. But this is not, of course, an empirical realism; Marx makes great play of the distinction between essence and appearance, insisting that 'all science would be superfluous if the outward appearance and the essence of things directly coincided.'

Derek Sayer has clearly identified the realist principles implicit in this distinction between phenomenal forms and real or essential relations.

Phenomenal forms are most simply defined as those forms in which the phenomena of the external world 'represent themselves' in people's experience. This does not imply either that human activity plays no role in constructing the world that thus presents itself, or that what is presented is not already conceptually mediated. It merely supposes that at any given point there exists a constituted world whose phenomena have achieved what Marx calls 'the stability of natural, self-understood forms of social life' and which in the first instance confronts its participants as a simple datum. Essential relations, in Marx's terminology, are those relations whose existence explains why phenomena should take such forms. They are essential, therefore, not in any mystical or immanentist sense, but simply as conditions of existence of the phenomenal forms themselves.

Unlike phenomenal forms, Marx holds, essential relations need not be transparent to direct experience. Phenomenal forms may be such as to mask or obscure the relations of which they are the forms of manifestation. Such divergence of forms and relations provides the basis for Marx's conception of ideology and at the same time defines the project of his science.[3]

Thus Marx begins *Capital* Volume 1 by analysing the phenomenal form of the commodity with its two components: use-value and exchange-value; the latter, he says, 'cannot be anything other than the mode of expression (*Ausdrucksweise*), the "form of appearance" (*Erscheinungsform*), of a content distinguishable from it.'[4] As Sayer shows, building on the brilliant analysis of I. I. Rubin,[5] the Hegelian language of Marx's mature work translates directly into a modern idiom of scientific realism, as developed by Hanson and Bhaskar.[6]

It would not be necessary to insist on Marx's realism were it not for the fact that influential commentators have forced Marx's more 'activist' formulations in the direction of a radical thesis of epistemic constitution in which it is human practice (including cognitive practice) which is responsible not just for the origins but for the validity of statements about the natural and social world.[7] I shall not repeat here my attempt in *Concept Formation in Social Science* to spell out the limits of this notion of constitution in terms of Bhaskar's distinction between transitive and intransitive objects of knowledge. Lukács's classic assertion, for example,[8] that nature is a social category is unproblematically, though interestingly true of the transitive domain of science, and utterly false if extended to the intransitive domain. (This is no less true of the social world than of the natural world; to say that society is a social category is false if this is understood to mean, as Simmel sometimes seems to imply, that it is merely a form of apperception.)[9] Rather, we make (or, rather, transform) the world through a variety of practices; conceptualising is not the most efficacious form of practice, though it is not without real effects.

There is, however, a more interesting set of qualifications in Marx as to the status of the structures and mechanisms which he identifies in the capitalist mode of production. Marx's criticism of political economy was in large part precisely that it failed to recognise the historicity of the processes which it described; many of its categories have a qualified validity within capitalism, but would cease to apply in a communist mode of production. In other words, the tendencies which Marx saw manifesting themselves with iron necessity in contemporary society would cease to do so to the extent that production was brought under rational social control. There is an analogy here, as Habermas has pointed out, with some of the causal mechanisms postulated by psychoanalytic theory, which lose their efficacy to the extent that they are 'seen through' and brought under control. (In Freud's slogan, 'Where the id was, the ego shall be'.) How far Marx's expectations in this respect were realistic is a question which lies outside the scope of this discussion; I have merely been concerned to show that his metatheory was a realist one.

To say this is not, of course, to say anything about Marx's scientific, as distinct from his philosophical, ontology; the former must take its chance on the terrain of theoretical, as opposed to metatheoretical criticism. But the discussion in the rest of this chapter of other social theorists will, I hope, convince the reader that, whatever the theoretical inadequacies of Marx's work, his (largely implicit) metatheory has considerable merits.[10] And it seems to me, though I shall not attempt to argue this here, that these metatheoretical virtues made an important contribution to the strengths of Marx's overall theory of society.[11]

It is well known that Durkheim was strongly influenced by the positivism of St-Simon and Comte; less attention has been paid to the other principal influence on his development: the neo-Kantian philosophy of Renouvier and others. For the purposes of this discussion, we can ignore the interplay of these influences in the development of Durkheim's thought and concentrate on the conception which was firmly established by the time he wrote the *Rules of Sociological Method*. What we are given in the *Rules* is a qualified realist ontology of social facts – qualified by Durkheim's occasional shifts from asserting the facticity of social or moral facts to recommending that we should treat them as things. In practice, however, Durkheim always gives a realist interpretation to his concepts – even when they are as prima facie suspect as the 'suicidogenic currents'.[12]

Durkheim's other basic principle, that arguments should be transcendental in form, does not appear explicitly in the *Rules*, except in the assertion that a social fact must be explained by another (antecedent) social fact.[13] What lies behind this is a characteristic form of transcendental argumentation: given that suicide exists in a regular geographical and social distribution, or that religion exists as a universal social fact, what might explain this? It is in *The Elementary Forms of Religious Life* that this argument appears in its most naked, because purely *a priori* form. Religion is clearly a mistake, in the sense that there are no supernatural entities, yet a social fact of such generality cannot be based *merely* on a mistake; what then could it be based on, if not society?[14] As Gillian Rose has pointed out this transcendental form of argumentation in part explains the apparent circularity of Durkheim's arguments: 'a transcendental account necessarily presupposes the actuality of existence of its object and seeks to discover the conditions of its possibility.'[15]

Now there are all kinds of criticisms to be made of Durkheim's sociological theorising – most fundamentally at the level of his social ontology, in which an 'oversocialised conception of society' dualistically confronts an equally reified conception of the individual. From the standpoint of a realist metatheory, however, the problems lie rather in the way his basically realist philosophical ontology is connected up with the empirical by means of his idiosyncratic conceptions of definition and causation.

Definitions, for Durkheim, must be based on common external characteristics; he assumes without argument that these will provide adequate access to the underlying phenomena to be investigated.[16] Thus his definition of suicide as an act which the actor knows will bring about his or her death provides Durkheim with an extremely mixed bag of acts which agents themselves would hardly classify in the same way.[17] Secondly, when Durkheim goes on to distinguish different types of suicide within this broad class, he is constrained to do so in terms of their alleged causes, given his highly counterintuitive belief that the same effect cannot be produced by different causes.[18] Here common sense and realism converge in the belief that an effect may in fact be brought about by a complex mixture of causal tendencies, located at different levels of reality (physiological, social, psychological). Thus when French people rush off to lunch at precisely 1200 hours, their action may be motivated, in varying degrees, by hunger, by social convention, by individual psychological obsessions about punctuality, and so forth. Durkheim, by contrast, ends up with an extremely dubious aetiological classification of types of suicide or, in the case of religion, with a speculative single cause-essence. Thus Durkheim's uneasy combination of realism and empiricism, which would hardly matter if it were merely an equivocation at the level of philosophical ontology, in fact leads Durkheim to formulate his explanation in an unconvincing and perhaps incoherent form. Max Weber, unlike Durkheim, upholds a basically anti-realist view of social scientific theory. For while sociology is or should be a *Wirklichkeitswissenschaft*, a science of concrete reality which seeks to identify 'general rules of what takes place',[19] Weber is sceptical about the grip of our concepts on social or natural reality. Realism for Weber is an 'antique-scholastic epistemology' which sees concepts as aiming at 'the reproduction of "objective" reality in the analyst's imagination.'[20]

Nothing, however, is more dangerous than the *confusion* of theory and history stemming from naturalistic prejudices. This confusion expresses itself firstly in the belief that the 'true' content and the essence of historical reality is portrayed in such theoretical constructs or secondly, in the use of these constructs as a procrustean bed into which history is to be forced or thirdly, in the hypostatization of such 'ideas' as real 'forces' and as a 'true' reality which operates behind the passage of events and which works itself out in history.[21]

Against this view Weber opposes 'the basic principle of the modern theory of knowledge which goes back to Kant', namely that 'concepts are primarily means of thought for the intellectual mastery of empirical data and can only be that.'[22] Together with Weber's neo-Kantian position on the complexity of empirical reality, this means that theoretical concepts can only be ideal types: 'Every concept which is not *purely* classificatory diverges from reality.'[23]

As in the case of Durkheim, we can get at the essentials of Weber's position by looking at his theories of concept formation and causality. In the passage cited above, Weber explicates his notion of the ideal type in terms of the contrast with 'purely classificatory' empirical concepts, using the example of the concepts 'church' and 'sect':

[These concepts] . . . may be broken down purely in classificatory fashion into complexes of elements [*Merkmalskomplexe*] whereby not only the distinction between them but also the content of each concept must constantly remain fluid. If, however, I wish to conceptualize 'sect' in a *genetic* fashion, e.g. in reference to certain important cultural significances which the 'sectarian spirit' has had for modern culture, certain characteristics of both become *essential* because they stand in an adequate causal relationship to those effects. However, the concepts thereupon become ideal-typical, i.e. in full conceptual purity these phenomena either do not exist at all or only in single instances. Here as elsewhere it is the case that every concept which is not *purely* classificatory diverges from reality.

Another example comes at the beginning of *Economy and Society*[24] where Weber distinguishes a 'conceptually constructed *pure* type of . . . subjectively *intended* meaning' from that which is 'in fact' present in a specific case or present as an approximate average in a class of cases.

This notion of the ideal or pure type was not of course peculiar to Weber; he seems to have taken it from Jellinek's *Allgemeine Staatslehre* of 1900, and it was common currency among many of his contemporaries, notably the philosopher Heinrich Rickert, the economist Carl Menger, and the sociologist-philosophers Ferdinand Tönnies and Georg Simmel. Weber's ideal types are however distinguished from those of the last two authors by the peculiar freedom he allows in their construction.[25] For Simmel, they are 'typical forms' *abstracted* from empirical reality and further grounded in more general philosophical and psychological speculations, and the last feature is also present in Tönnies's concepts of *Gemeinschaft* and *Gesellschaft* which he grounds in a psychological metaphysics of the will.

Weber's ideal types, by contrast, are grounded in a radicalised (because subjectivised) version of Rickert's notion of value-reference (*Wertbeziehung*); this links together the influence on the social scientist of general cultural values and his or her more personal and pragmatic concerns in a given piece of research. The influence of cultural values à la Rickert is best illustrated by the introduction to Weber's sociology of religion, where he claims that 'A product of modern European civilization . . . is bound to ask himself to what combination of circumstances the fact should be attributed that in Western civilisation, and in Western civilisation only, cultural phenomena have appeared which (as we like to think) lie in a line of development having *universal* significance and value.' The more specific impulses of the social scientist can be seen in the stipulative definitions at the beginning of *Economy and Society*, of which Weber said:

> In *my* theory of concepts the claim is this: for particular methodical purposes *I* define these structures in this way – and only the scientific pay-off (*Ertrag*) will justify my procedure.[26]

In both of these cases, the point is the same:

> *There is no* absolutely 'objective' scientific analysis of culture or
> . . . of 'social phenomena' *independent* of special and 'one-sided' view-points according to which – expressly or tacitly, consciously or unconsciously – they are selected, analysed and organised for expository purposes.[27]

Weber's theory of causality is simply a corollary of this account of ideal types. The problem as Weber sees it is not, *pace* Hume, that there are no causal connections in reality, but that there are too many of them for us to handle. We therefore have to select some of them, and selection here involves both the focusing on a particular link or set of links in a causal chain and the simplification of the relations in that chain itself. The establishment of one or more such simplified sequences provides us with approximation to the real causal relations, which are in a strict sense unknowable in virtue of their complexity. As Weber put it, 'In order to gain insight into the real [*wirklich*] causal connections, *we construct unreal ones.*'[28]

The problem with Weber's analysis of ideal types can be simply stated if we ask what could lead a social scientist to abandon an ideal type. Weber has only two answers to give: one in terms of the pragmatics of research, the second in terms of cultural history. The pragmatic answer is implicit in his remarks cited above from Marianne Weber's biography: what counts is the 'scientific pay-off'. Ideal-types are not hypotheses, but means to the construction of hypotheses,[29] and the latter may, Weber assumes, be refuted or confirmed by evidence. But even if he is right about the possibility of refutation, it is not clear how this might force us to abandon the ideal-type which contributed to a rejected hypothesis: the former can survive the demise of the latter. Alternatively, the ideal-types may be compared more directly with empirical reality, as when a pure type of rational economic action serves as a standard from which to judge empirical deviations from it. But Weber can only sustain this possibility of comparison by smuggling back in a notion of direct access to reality which he has undermined by his doctrine of value-relevance.

Weber's cultural-historical account of the rise and fall of ideal types merely exacerbates the problem. On this model, ideal-types are dropped because we lose interest in the conceptual issues which they address.

> There comes a moment when the atmosphere changes. . . . The light of the great cultural problems moves on. Then science too prepares to change its standpoint and its analytical apparatus.[30]

Hence

> The greatest advances in the sphere of the social sciences are substantially tied up with the shift in practical cultural problems and take the guise of a critique of concept-construction.[31]

But unless there is a Hegelian cunning of reason embedded in the 'cultural problems', it is not clear how we can know that we have 'advanced'. To sustain this possibility, Weber is forced to postulate a reality which is knowable independently of theoretical concepts and with which rival concepts can be compared. It may be argued that this is a problem for any theory of science, but Weber's peculiarly subjectivistic account of ideal-typical concept-formation does not really help us to confront these issues. Like Pascal, who said that nothing is freer than definitions, Weber tells us that nothing is freer than ideal-type construction; it is enough for us to be guided in our use of them by our 'sensitivity' or 'tact' with regard to empirical reality; concepts which survive this confrontation with empirical reality may or may not survive the longer-term process of cultural evolution in our societies.

Weber's intentions are clear enough; he wishes to combine the subjectivity of orientations in social or cultural science with objective criteria for judging its results. He emphatically denies that the investigations in the cultural sciences can only . . . have *results* which are 'subjective' in the sense that they are *valid* for one person and not valid for another. What changes is rather the degree to which they *interest* one and not the other. In other words: *whatever* becomes the object of investigation . . . is determined by the value-ideas dominating the scientist and his time; but as to the 'How?', the method of investigation . . . the scientist, of course, here as everywhere is bound to the norms of out thinking.[32]

But even if we are prepared to share Weber's optimism about objective evaluation of scientific 'results', the problem with the ideal-type concepts is precisely that they teeter between the sphere of results and the sphere of value-related interests. Weber would like to see them purely as *means*, but he cannot do so without falling back into a kind of empiricism.

Finally, it is worth looking briefly at Talcott Parsons, whose work is relevant to the present discussion in two important ways. First, Parsons needs to be understood as a transcendental thinker who runs together, in a peculiarly intricate way, the possibility of social science and the possibility of social order; this theory of normatively regulated social action is intended to answer both of these questions.[33] Utilitarian theories (in which Parsons rather implausibly includes Marxism) fail both at a theoretical level to account for the ends of human action and, at a more substantive level, to explain the basis of social order without the 'untenable' postulate of the natural harmony of individual interests.[34] Parsons's notoriously equivocal use of the phrase 'normative orientation of action' is the semantic expression of this double focus; it operates (a) as a theoretical principle to explain choices between alternative projects of action and thus to get over the utilitarian-economic problem with the randomness of ends and (b) as a guarantee of social order, where 'normative' means 'oriented towards a system of socially dominant values'. Parsons himself oscillates between a recognition of the transcendental status of his theory, as where he compares the action frame of reference to the space–time framework of Newtonian physics and Kantian philosophy, and an alternative 'modern' conception of science, where his theory is seen as a hypothetico-deductive schema open to empirical testing. Despite Parsons's efforts with Bales and others in the latter direction, he never succeeded in making plausible this second conception of the status of his theory.

The second element of Parsons's theory which is relevant here is his metatheory of 'analytical realism', in which

> it is maintained that at least some of the general concepts of science are not fictional but adequately 'grasp' aspects of the objective external world. This is true of the concepts here called analytical elements. Hence the position here taken is, in an empirical sense, realistic. At the same time it avoids the objectionable implications of an empiricist realism. These concepts correspond, not to concrete phenomena, but to elements in them which are analytically separable from other elements. There is no implication that the value of any one such element, or even of all those included in any one logically coherent system, is completely descriptive of any particular concrete thing or event.[35]

From a realist point of view, Parsons is right to reject empiricism and 'fictionalism', yet in the end his realism remains, as Schnädelbach said of Karl Popper, 'methodologically without consequence'. In the end the influence of positivistic philosophy of science leads Parsons away from developing a realist ontology of the social and towards a conception where discrete 'analytic' sciences (sociology, economics, psychology etc.) are responsible for distinct areas of concrete social life.[36] This step has both metatheoretical and theoretical consequences which are disastrous to Parsons's project. Metatheoretically, it means that, whether or not he chooses to give a realistic interpretation of particular analytical sciences,[37] his account of the totality of these sciences as they bear on concrete social reality can only become conventionalist in character. The significance of this metatheoretical shift becomes clear in its theoretical consequences: an *apartheid* system of distinct sciences defined in a more or less arbitrary manner – economics in terms of resource allocation, sociology in terms of the maintenance of social solidarity and so on. But, as Burger points out, this is to commit

> what Polanyi . . . has called the 'economistic fallacy', namely the assumption of a natural link between a certain type of action and

a particular social function. . . . [This is a fallacy because] the
provision of men with goods may be accomplished by actions not
at all guided by economic considerations . . . . This shows that
there are not intrinsic relations between the economic aspects of
concrete phenomena, and that an analytic economics therefore
cannot describe such connections. Naturally the same objection
must be raised against an analytic sociology. The war of all
against all may be avoided by all sorts of means; the social
function of coherence is not 'intrinsically' accomplished by being
'moral' or 'solidarizing'.[38]

In other words, Parsons's substantive sociological claim that the
basis of social order is exclusively normative rather than a product
of 'the interrelations between the phenomena of self-interested
exchange, domination and normative conviction',[39] rests on an
unargued assumption about the intrinsic character of the analytic
science of sociology – itself grounded in turn in positivistic
assumptions about the relationship between a science and its
objects. Durkheim's ghost is present in Parsons's metatheory as
much as in his substantive theory.

Here then is a further example of the intricate way in which an
apparently innocuous metatheoretical assumption about the
relationship between a science and its object-domain came to skew
an entire substantive sociological or economic theory in a particular
direction.[40] Parsons is not often accused of oversimplification, yet
this seems to be the case with his analytical divisions between the
social sciences; conversely, the apparently banal claims made in
transcendental realism, at the level of philosophical ontology,
about the complex stratification of all reality, including social
reality, can point the way to a more adequate conception of the
interrelations between the social sciences.[41]

The upshot of this critique is that questions of social ontology
must be tackled head-on and not hived off to a set of discrete social
sciences which claim to be individually rigorous and jointly
exhaustive of social reality. The most promising way to avoid such
reification, I believe, is to look at individual action in a
hermeneutically more sensitive manner than that of Parsons's
voluntaristic theory of action. In the next chapter I shall attempt to
draw together some of the implications of the metatheoretical

themes touched on earlier in this book and to relate them to contemporary theorising about 'action' and 'structure' in social reality.

7

Conclusion: Action, Structure and Realist Philosophy

The crucial issue for realist naturalism is the sense to be given to structural concepts in the social sciences. Unlike reductionist forms of positivist naturalism, which tend to be attracted by behaviourism, a realist naturalism emphasises the stratification of reality as a general metaphysical principle. In the form defended here, it also accepts the 'hermeneutic' principle that the concepts and theories of the social sciences must make substantial reference to those of actors in the life-world. At the centre of our social ontology there must be, then, the commonsense picture of physically distinct persons capable of independent action: what Harré and Secord ironically called 'the anthropomorphic model of man'.[1]

With a little more elaboration, this becomes the collection of analytic truths which Steven Lukes calls 'Truistic Social Atomism':

> Society consists of people. Groups consist of people. Institutions consist of people plus rules and roles. Rules are followed (or alternatively not followed) by people and roles are filled by people. Also there are traditions, customs, ideologies, kinship systems, languages: these are ways people act, think and talk.[2]

Methodological individualists, of course, turn this into a non-trivial reductionist thesis cast in ontological and/or explanatory terms.

As I suggested in my previous book,[3] sociological conceptions of society can usefully be classified in terms of a modified Bhaskarian distinction between empirical realism, transcendental idealism and transcendental realism. Empiricists either insist on a reductionist analysis of concepts such as society or social structure or, in an empirical realist mode, they treat society as an empirically given, self-subsistent entity on the basis of biological or system analogies. Transcendental idealist theories, rejecting this type of holism, reconceptualise society as an abstract principle of sociation (*Vergesellschaftung*), realised in the actions and perceptions of individuals. Finally, for transcendental realism, 'society is both the ever-present *condition* (material cause) and the continually produced *outcome* of human agency.'[4]

Before looking at concepts of social structure in more detail, we must note a further tendency within social theory to identify the 'action' level with freedom and the 'structure' or 'system' level with constraint. (To paraphrase Marx's first thesis on Feuerbach, the active side was developed by individualism.) Theories of *collective* praxis can be found here and there, from Marx to Sartre and Touraine,[5] but they are very much a minority. They are also somewhat threatened by the currently fashionable attempts by Olson, Roemer, Elster, and others to explicate the logic of collective action in individualist terms.[6]

The opposition between 'action' and 'system' or 'structure' is one of the most pervasive in the whole tradition of social theory. Alan Dawe puts the issue very clearly:

> In a sociology of social system, then, social actors are pictured as being very much at the receiving end of the social system. In terms of their existence and nature as social beings, their social behaviour and relationships, and their very sense of personal identity as human beings, they are determined by it. The process is one whereby they are socialised into society's central values and into the norms appropriate to the roles they are to play in the division of labour. Social action is thus entirely the product and derivative of social system.`
>
> In total opposition to this, a sociology of social action conceptualises the social system as the derivative of social action and interaction, a social world produced by its members, who are thus pictured as active, purposeful, self- and socially-creative beings.[7]

It is clear that these 'two sociologies' resonate with a variety of other social concerns, for example with the opposition between liberal and anarchist political theories on the one hand, and fascism or Stalinism on the other. More fundamentally still, they may be seen to express a fundamental dualism in human attitudes to reality. Some of the time we feel free, independent and creative in our social life; at other times we feel oppressed by 'our station and its duties'. Or, changing the signs, we may feel terrorised by our sense of existential freedom and lapse into Sartrean bad faith, the warm reassurance of unquestioned social routines. Against this background, the attempt to mediate this opposition at the level of social theory and methodology may seem misplaced. And yet any adequate social theory must surely addresss our intuition that, for example, in writing this book I am less constrained in my actions than someone doing forced labour at gunpoint.

The first step is to recognise what Giddens has termed the 'duality of structure':

> Structures must not be conceptualised as simply placing constraints upon human agency, but as enabling . . . . Structures can always in principle be examined in terms of their *structuration* as a series of reproduced practices. To enquire into the structuration of practices is to seek to explain how it comes about that structures are constituted through action, and reciprocally how action is constituted structurally.[8]

More concretely, this involves recognising 'that the concept of action is logically linked to that of power, if the latter is interpreted in a broad sense as the capability of achieving outcomes'.[9] Giddens suggests analysing power in terms of 'resources':

> Resources are drawn upon by actors in the production of interaction, but are constituted as structures of domination. Resources are the media whereby power is employed in the routine course of social action; but they are at the same time structural elements of social systems, reconstituted in social interaction. Social systems are constituted as regularised practices, reproduced across time and space; power and space: power in social systems can thus be treated as involving reproduced relations of *autonomy and dependence* in social interaction. (Ibid.)

Here then is a plausible attempt to reconceptualise the relations between action and structure in social life.[10] How might a realist metatheory bear on this and other theoretical approaches? As I have argued throughout this book, and especially in Chapter 3, it is a mistake to move directly from metatheory to substantive theory, to offer a spurious metatheoretical warrant for a particular form of theory. At the same time, however, a realist position clearly raises the stakes in the opposition between structure and agency. In insisting on a realistic interpretation, it may increase the temptation to reduce one to the other.

The reduction of agency to structure, or of agents to 'bearers' of structures, has been rightly identified as a central problem in Althusser's reformulation of Marxism, but John Urry has suggested in various texts that it may be a danger inherent in a realist interpretation of Marxism or, for that matter, of any other social theory.[11] In the case of Marxism, the production and appropriation of surplus-value is construed as the underlying mechanism which

gives rise to prices, wages, profits, interest, rent and so on, the phenomenal forms. However, such a conception is problematic in two respects. First, it may lead to viewing such societies as characterised by an 'expressive totality', that *all* aspects or elements of it are merely the phenomenal forms of the inner essence or mechanism. And second, no account is provided of the precise kinds of practice which individuals would have to engage in, so that these phenomenal forms are generated. Many aspects of capitalist society are not unmediated expressions of its central mechanism; they result from the forms of social practice and struggle in which individual subjects are forced to engage.[12]

These are real defects, but they seem to me to be defects in Marxism,[13] and more particularly in certain modern interpretations of it, notably those of the West German 'capital logicians' (who are not to my knowledge enthusiasts for realism), rather than problems inherent in realist metatheory as such. The remedy lies in part in Urry's own no less realist analysis of 'the social space in which individual subjectivities are constituted and reproduced, the differing forms and effectivity of social struggle, and the character of the state.'[14]

The opposite tendency to dissolve structures into action and interaction may seem a more natural consequence of a realist position. Realism in the natural sciences has often been based on the alleged reality of the entities postulated by scientific theories, rather than the truth of the theories themselves. Theories about the electron come and go, but we know too much about electrons, and are too skilled in manipulating them to doubt their reality. In Ian Hacking's phrase: 'if you can spray them then they're real.'[15] But do we really want to talk this way about 'entities' such as the Protestant economic ethic, Bourdieu's *habitus*, Freud's unconscious, and so on? Should we not rather be talking, with Rom Harré, about societal icons?

According to the view which I wish to advocate, society and the institutions within a society are not to be conceived as independent existents, *of* which we conceive icons. Rather, they *are* icons which are described in explanations of certain problematic situations. Thus, the *concept* of a Trade Union, or a University, is to be treated as a theoretical concept judged by its explanatory power, rather than a descriptive concept judged by its conformity to an independent reality. The form of a social and a scientific explanation are identical, but their ontological commitments and metaphysical structures are quite different. Beyond the icons of reality which are conceived for purposes of explanation in the natural sciences, lies a real world of active things; but beyond the icons conceived for the explanation of social interactions by social actions lies nothing but those very actors, their conformative behaviour and their ideas.[16]

Thus for Harré, class theory

describes a well-known image or icon. It is not a theory which describes an independent reality, and it is the basis of a wide variety of explanations in terms of which various differences between people can be made intelligible . . . Now it is my contention that classes exist only insofar as they are thought to exist and the function of such a notion is to provide a standard, ready-made, easily acceptable explanation for understanding what has happened on some occasion.[17]

The problem with this line of argument is that unless the terms 'explanation', 'intelligible', 'easily acceptable' all refer to nothing more than what counts in a given community, we need criteria for what is a good explanation, and this in turn requires some conception of a reality which is (mostly) independent of the way we perceive and explain it. As I argued in Chapter 3, Harré is right to insist on (1) the bedrock status of individual social actions and on (2) the open-ended quality of theoretical interpretation in the social sciences, but this does not mean that all non-naive explanations must be in terms of concrete actions or that 'anything goes' for icon-construction in the social domain. Harré's first point seems to be met by Bhaskar's formulation that 'social structures, unlike natural structures, do not exist independently of the activities they govern . . . [and] . . . of the agents' conception of what they are doing in their activity.'[18] Indeed this formulation may go too far in the direction of reducing structures; we need to include counterfactual references to action. To say that I occupy a position of power may mean that I actually exercise power or that I could do so if I chose to.

The second point, the open-ended character of social theory, I discussed at some length in Chapter 2. To cast the discussion in terms of realism about entities is, I think, to commit the fallacy of misplaced concreteness. It is clear that the entities postulated by social science are different from those postulated by natural science, but the interesting issues are not here but rather in the global differences between the activity of theorising in the two domains and, in particular, in the much lesser revelatory power of social theory. To give up on the aspiration that social science can ever furnish 'the same kind of sensational illumination and explanatory power already yielded up by the sciences of nature'[19] is not to deny *any* explanatory power to social theory. Nor does it commit us to saying, with Bourdieu, that all explanatory statements in the social sciences must be preceded by the qualifying statement that 'everything happens as if . . .'[20]

A brief discussion of action theory and methodological individualism may help us to clarify these issues. The main thrust of the realist critique of positivistic and neo-Kantian metatheory is against their tendency to reduce ontology to epistemology and both of these ultimately to methodology. It seems to me, however, that once we have correctly understood the terms of the ontological relations between action and structure, along the lines of Giddens's conception of the 'duality of structure' and Bhaskar's 'transformational model of social activity', we can see the issues of action-theoretical and individualistic reduction for what they are: namely, methodological questions about appropriate levels of abstraction, governed in each case by the pragmatics of the research process. In other words, if it is right to say that the action frame of reference is 'just that approach of penetrating deeper, and with greater precision, into the way society exists only in individuals in definite social relations',[21] this is not because structures are unreal and only action theory has a legitimate foundation in a basic Strawsonian ontology of persons,[22] but because, for certain purposes, this is the appropriate level of abstraction at which to operate.

It is of course not only a matter of methodology, given the ontological relationship between structure and action, but these two dimensions of methodology and ontology can and must be held apart. Methodological individualism needs to be seen as just that, a method which is appropriate in some contexts and not in others; the confusion arises because individualists have tried to go further and to ground their methodological programme in an empirical realist ontology, symbolised by terms like 'bedrock', 'rock bottom explanation', and so on. (The ideological smear that anyone who opposes methodological individualism is logically committed to a contempt for the individual which leads to the construction of concentration camps has merely compounded the confusion.) The substantive issues of individualism versus holism are immensely wide-ranging and cannot be dealt with here, but it is important to block off this tendency to confuse methodology and philosophy. In an excellent recent book, Susan James has shown that the methodological opposition between individualism and holism needs to be disentangled from an inconsequential philosophical dispute about the possibility of reducing statements about social structures to statements about individuals. As James shows, to situate the argument at this level is to neglect the diversity of social theories and the different intellectual (explanatory) interests which they aim to satisfy.

By concentrating on the notion of reduction, [the traditional debate] misses a deeper and more important divide: holism and individualism are based on competing views about the nature of individuals, each of which gives rise to a distinctive account of how to explain the social world. In the light of this insight the problem can be seen afresh. Rather than having to do with the various criteria for the reducibility of theories, it is concerned with the relationship between, and comparative power of, two kinds of causal analysis: those that appeal to the properties of social wholes to account for the features of individuals on the one hand, and those that seek to explain the characteristics of social wholes as the outcome of individual traits on the other.[23]

James thus shows that the dispute between holism and individualism is 'a dispute between equal parties', guided by the different interests with which they approach a given subject matter. Thus even when the side-issues of reductionism on the one hand and ideological suspicion on the other are excluded from the dispute, it remains the case that individualists are left unsatisfied by explanations in terms of social wholes – whether they see them as involving the illegitimate reification of abstract entities, or merely as incomplete explanation-sketches. Conversely, holists are left unsatisfied by explanations which stress the autonomous choices made by individuals, arguing that these choices are causally unimportant and that what *are* important are the structural pressures which shape the actions of individuals, whoever they may happen to be.

This is not the place to examine in detail the ways in which the rival poles of holism and individualism exercise their attraction on particular social theorists, either in general or in specific aspects of their work. The forms taken by individualist and holistic explanations are too diverse to allow any simple principle of classification. What is I think clear, is that individualist forms of explanation need to be assessed on their merits rather than in terms of some general reductionist thesis grounded in an empiricist ontology. It is clear that human individuals have a special ontological status in social theory. In Barry Hindess's neat formulation, 'Human individuals may not be the constitutive subjects of social life, but they are the only actors whose actions do not invariably involve the actions of others.'[24]

This must be recognised, as must the fact that structural concepts such as class are 'theoretical' and open to dispute. But nothing much follows from this in terms of explanatory primacy. Many of the more interesting explanations in history and the social sciences, if they are to be possible at all, must take a holistic form, in the sense that an insistence on individualistic reduction can only seem impossibly perverse. To explain the secular decline in the value of the pound sterling in terms of the individual decisions of foreign exchange dealers is as sensible as to explain a wet August in Britain by plotting the trajectories of rain-drops. (Conversely where, as often in conventional economic theory, the reference is to 'the' typical individual, one may question whether this is really an individualist form of explanation in any serious sense.)[25]

To take another example which I have used elsewhere, discrimination in employment is in the last instance a product of individual or collective decisions to hire, fire, promote, etc. It is therefore a matter of some interest to investigate why individual employers may prefer white/male/middle-class applicants to equally qualified black/female/working-class ones. But such an investigation at the point of discrimination will not tell us anything interesting about the more systematic processes of exclusion operating through the mechanisms of an educational system which is ostensibly open to all. These processes can of course themselves be investigated in detail, but from the point of view of a study of job discrimination they operate as fundamental structural conditions which cannot be left out of the explanation.

Here, as elsewhere, the essential point is that the social sciences require a plurality of methodological approaches, no less than do the natural sciences. The merits of these approaches can only be judged in the practice of these sciences and the extent to which they seem, to social scientists and to the public, to enrich our understanding of the social world. The residual truth of anti-naturalist conceptions of the social sciences is the recognition that they are inescapably bound up with our non-scientific thinking about and acting in the human societies of which we are members. This recognition sets inevitable limits to reductionist scientistic theories of the social which efface the distinction between social and non-social systems. Most sociological theory has always been aware of this, but the great gain of the last two decades has, I think, been the sharpening of this awareness via the impact of analytic philosophy of language and continental European hermeneutics. The time has now come, I think, to build on these insights in the ways in which Habermas, Bourdieu, Giddens and others have done. And it seems to me that a realist philosophy of science and a qualified or critical naturalism provides the best metatheoretical framework for further development. To say this is not to say that there is nothing to be learned from social theories which are radically anti-naturalistic or which reject a realist metatheory as wrong or irrelevant. As in the case of the natural sciences, the metatheoretical attachments of a particular theory will often, indeed turn out to be irrelevant to its explanatory power and the interest of its conclusions – in which case their investigation can safely be left to historians of ideas. Often, however, a philosophical metatheory does have substantive consequences. In Chapter 6 I attempted to demonstrate some of these consequences for classical sociology; the influence of positivism on the more recent developments in sociology and the other social sciences can hardly be denied. In economics, one can demonstrate the support given to neoclassical theory, as opposed to classical or Marxist alternatives, by the unquestioned shibboleths of positivist conventionalism.[26] Such assumptions have also been particularly strong in psychology and provided what from a realist point of view are bad reasons for the rejection of psychoanalytic theory.[27] The strength of positivist influence has been extremely variable: strong in political science and linguistics,[28] much weaker in social anthropology. History, as I suggested in Chapter 1, has on the whole escaped the direct influence of positivist theories of explanation, but it remains somewhat in thrall to an empiricist suspicion of all forms of theory and a fetishisation of primary sources.

Now it may be that we would be better off without such realist forms of theory as Marxian economics, Freudian psychoanalysis, Chomskyan linguistics, and so forth, but it is important that they should not be ruled out of court by a philosophical dogma, especially one which is somewhat eclipsed within philosophy itself. Many recent realist contributions such as those cited in the previous paragraph have so far been primarily concerned to reopen these issues; the positive effects of a philosophical milieu imbued with realist rather than positivist principles will be slow to appear and hard to identify with precision, but I think they will be none the less real.[29]

The above discussion raises once again the question of the

relationships between philosophy and the social sciences. The preceding chapters should have made clear that these relationships have been both very close and enormously varied. As I stressed at the outset, one of the peculiarities of the 'new realism' is the unusually close relationship between philosophical and sociological problematics. This combination of philosophy and social theory was felt to be interesting and relevant because it arrived on the scene after a prolonged period of theoretical (and, increasingly, metatheoretical) uncertainty in sociology, and, to a much lesser extent, the other social sciences. This opening towards philosophy was of course only part of a general questioning of disciplinary boundaries, but what is interesting is how far it went in the areas of philosophy of science, philosophy of language and, for some, right back to the pre-Socratics. In someone's pithy phrase, British sociological theory threatened to disappear up Wittgenstein's backside. Amid this explosion of work on the borders of philosophy and the social sciences, it is easy to lose sight of the more subterranean, but no less powerful philosophical influences on earlier generations of social scientists, where the power of the positivist consensus lay in its ability to brand alternative philosophical systems as irremediably old-fashioned.

Some critics of realist philosophy of science have accused it of similarly totalitarian aspirations, especially when it generates naturalistic prescriptions for the social sciences.[30] As I have argued throughout this book, however, the realist claim is not that any particular science, in its present configuration, has indeed captured objective structures of natural or social reality, but merely that it is meaningful and pragmatically useful to posit the existence of such structures as *possible* objects of scientific description. Once again, the affinity of realism to pragmatism, and its opposition to more prescriptive philosophical theories, is manifest in its insistence that the work of adjudicating between alternative descriptions is basically a matter for the individual sciences and, to varying degrees, the lay public.

The latter qualification is important, since realism is not committed to the adulatory reification of particular existing sciences, as intellectual and social forms, any more than to that of particular theories and methods within them. Its claim is the weaker but important one that ontological commitments, whether of general epistemologies or of specific scientific theories, are inescapable and to be taken seriously. It is in this sense that Bhaskar seems to me right to claim that realism is a philosophy *for* science, including the social sciences. There is here an inescapable *political* commitment to the overall project of modern science to expand and refine our knowledge of the natural and social world. If, as seems increasingly probable, the ultimate consequence of some elements of this project will be the extinction of human life, and most animal life, on our planet, it will of course be revealed as a complete disaster. But what else can we do? For all its elitism, conservatism and political irresponsibility, modern science, in the broadest sense of systematic study, and a politics informed by that study, is the only way we can hope to understand and retain some influence over the development of our societies.

References

Introduction

1. See William Outhwaite, 'Laws and Explanations in Sociology', in John Hughes *et al.* (eds), *Classical Disputes in Sociology* (London: Allen & Unwin, 1987).
2. Theodor Abel, 'The Operation Called *Verstehen*', *American Journal of Sociology*, vol. 54, 1948.
3. Christopher Bryant, *Positivism in Social Theory and Research* (London: Macmillan, 1985).
4. Peter Halfpenny, *Positivism and Sociology* (London: Allen & Unwin, 1982).
5. Anthony Giddens, 'Positivism and its Critics', in his *Studies in Social and Political Thought* (London: Hutchinson, 1977).
6. Tom Bottomore, *Marxist Sociology* (London: Macmillan, 1974).
7. Derek Sayer, *Marx's Method* (Brighton: Harvester, 1979).

1 Philosophies of Social Science: The Old and the New

1. Halfpenny, *Positivism and Sociology*.
2. H. T. Buckle, *History of Civilisation in England*, vol. 1, ch. 1 (London: 1899) (1st edn 1857).
3. William Outhwaite, *Understanding Social Life*, 2nd edn (Lewes: Jean Stroud, 1986) ch. 2 and *passim*.
4. Outhwaite, 'Laws and Explanations in Sociology'.
5. Otto Neurath, *Empiricism and Sociology* (Dordrecht: Reidel, 1973).
6. A typical example is Richard Rudner, *The Philosophy of Social Science* (Englewood Cliffs, NJ: Prentice Hall, 1966).
7. Karl Popper, *The Logic of Scientific Discovery* (London: Hutchinson, 1959), p. 59.
8. C. G. Hempel, 'The Function of General Laws in History', *Journal of Philosophy* vol. 39, 1942, pp. 35–48; reprinted in P. Gardiner (ed.), *Theories of History* (New York: Free Press, 1959), pp. 344–56.
9. Hempel, 'The Function of General Laws in History', in Gardiner (ed.), *Theories of History*, p. 352.
10. Ibid., pp. 349 f.
11. Michael Scriven, 'Truisms as the Grounds for Historical Explanations', p. 448, in Gardiner, *Theories of History*, pp. 443–75.

12. Ibid., p. 454.
13. Edmund Mokrzycki, *Philosophy of Science and Sociology* (London: Routledge & Kegan Paul, 1983), p. 65.
14. Ibid., p. 4.
15. See William Outhwaite, *Concept Formation in Social Science* (London: Routledge & Kegan Paul, 1983), especially p. 6.
16. Martin Hollis and Edward Nell, *Rational Economic Man* (Cambridge: Cambridge University Press, 1975).
17. Outhwaite, *Concept Formation in Social Science.*
18. Alfred Schutz, 'Choice and the Social Sciences', in L. Embree (ed.), *Life World and Consciousness* (Evanston: Northwestern University Press, 1972), especially p. 583. Cf. Outhwaite, *Concept Formation*, p. 65; Richard Grathoff (ed.), *The Theory of Social Action* (Indianapolis: Indiana University Press, 1978).
19. Peter Winch: *The Idea of a Social Science and its Relation to Philosophy* (London: Routledge & Kegan Paul, 1958), p. 123.
20. Karl-Otto Apel, *Analytic Philosophy of Language and the Geisteswissenschaften* (Dordrecht: Reidel, 1967), p. 2.
21. See John Thompson, *Critical Hermeneutics* (Cambridge: Cambridge University Press, 1981).
22. Jürgen Habermas, *Knowledge and Human Interests* (London: Heinemann, 1971).
23. T. Adorno *et al.*, *The Positivist Dispute in German Sociology* (London: Heinemann, 1976); Anthony Giddens (ed.), *Positivism and Sociology* (London: Heinemann, 1974).
24. T. S. Kuhn, *The Structure of Scientific Revolutions*, 2nd edn (Chicago: University of Chicago Press, 1970), p. 118.
25. Alisdair MacIntyre, *The Unconscious. A Conceptual Analysis* (London: Routledge & Kegan Paul, 1958).
26. Karl Popper, 'Normal Science and its Dangers', in Imre Lakatos and Alan Musgrave (eds), *Criticism and the Growth of Knowledge* (Cambridge: Cambridge University Press, 1970), p. 52.
27. Ibid., p. 57.
28. Mary Hesse, *Models and Analogies in Science* (Notre Dame: University of Notre Dame Press, 1963); *The Structure of Scientific Inference* (London: Macmillan, 1974).
29. R. Harré and E. H. Madden, *Causal Powers* (Oxford: Blackwell, 1975).

2 The Realist Alternative

1. In the language of transcendental philosophy, we 'constitute' the world by fitting it into hypothetical structures of description and explanation. See Outhwaite, *Concept Formation*, ch. 3.
2. Roy Bhaskar, *A Realist Theory of Science*, 2nd edn (Brighton, Harvester, 1978), p. 250.
3. *Auguste Comte and Positivism*, 2nd edn (London: 1866), p. 6, cited in Bhaskar, *A Realist Theory of Science*, p. 63.
4. P. A. Schlipp (ed.), *The Philosophy of Rudolf Carnap*, The Library of Living Philosophers, vol. 11 (New York: Tudor Press, 1963), p. 18.
5. Halfpenny, *Positivism and Sociology*, p. 108.

122 References

6. W. V. O. Quine, *From a Logical Point of View* (Cambridge, Mass.: Harvard University Press, 1953), pp. 41 f.
7. D. Davidson and J. Hintikka (eds), *Words and Objections* (Dordrecht: Reidel, 1969), p. 293. Cf. *Word and Object* (Cambridge, Mass.: MIT Press, 1960), p. 22.
8. Ibid.
9. Richard Rorty, *Philosophy and the Mirror of Nature* (Princeton, NJ: Princeton University Press, 1979), p. 151.
10. See, for example, David Papineau, *For Science in the Social Sciences* (London: Macmillan, 1978); Baas van Fraassen, *The Scientific Image* (Oxford: Clarendon Press, 1980).
11. See W. S. Newton-Smith, 'The Power of Scientific Rationality', *Fundamenta Scientiae*, vol. 7, nos 3/4, 1987.
12. See, for example, Nicholas Rescher, *Methodological Pragmatism* (Oxford: Blackwell, 1977).
13. Herbert Schnädelbach, *Erfahrung, Begründung und Reflexion. Versuch über den Positivismus* (Frankfurt: Suhrkamp, 1971), p. 9.
14. Halfpenny, *Positivism and Sociology*, p. 120.
15. W. F. Sellars, *Science, Perception and Reality* (London: Routledge & Kegan Paul, 1963).
16. Ibid., p. 97.
17. Hilary Putnam, *Meaning and the Moral Sciences* (London: Routledge & Kegan Paul, 1978), p. 24.
18. Mary Hesse, *Revolutions and Reconstructions in the Philosophy of Science* (Brighton, Harvester, 1980), pp. xviii and xix.
19. Ibid., p. 174.
20. Karl Popper, *Unended Quest. An Intellectual Autobiography* (Glasgow: Fontana/Collins, 1976), p. 150. *Logik der Forschung* is of course the book translated as *The Logic of Scientific Discovery*.
21. Popper, *Realism and the Aim of Science* (London: Hutchinson, 1983), p. 81.
22. See, for example, Sellars, *Science, Perception and Reality* and J. J. C. Smart, *Philosophy and Scientific Realism* (London: Routledge & Kegan Paul, 1963).
23. D.-H. Ruben, *Marxism and Materialism*, 2nd edn (Brighton: Harvester, 1979), p. 102.
24. Ibid., p. 101.
25. Objective idealism of a Hegelian kind, it seems, rather than a subjective idealism based on perception (ibid., p. 107).
26. Ibid., p. 108.
27. Ibid., p. 104.
28. Ibid., p. 109.
29. Bhaskar, *A Realist Theory of Science*, p. 9; cf. p. 20.
30. Ibid., p. 29.
31. For the programme, see Otto Neurath, *Empiricism and Sociology* (Dordrecht and Boston: Reidel, 1973) and, for a history of philosophy based on this conception, Hans Reichenbach, *The Rise of Scientific Philosophy* (Berkeley: University of California Press, 1951).
32. Ruben, *Marxism and Materialism*, p. 99.
33. Bhaskar, *A Realist Theory of Science*, pp. 24 ff.
34. Richard Rorty, *Consequences of Pragmatism* (Brighton: Harvester, 1982), p. xxvi.
35. Ibid., p. 249.
36. Ibid., p. 248.

37. I shall argue later that it must also be made in the social world, though here the more fundamental role of hermeneutics requires that the realist position must be somewhat qualified.
38. T. S. Kuhn, 'The Function of Dogma in Scientific Research', in A. C. Crombie (ed.), *Scientific Change* (London: Heinemann, 1963).
39. Bhaskar, *A Realist Theory of Science*, p. 43.
40. Herbert Schnädelbach, 'Uber den Realismus', *Zeitschrift für allgemeine Wissenschaftstheorie*, vol. 3, no. 1, 1972, p. 95.
41. Martin Hollis, *Models of Man* (Cambridge: Cambridge University Press, 1977); Deryck Beyleveld, 'Epistemological Foundations of Sociological Theory', Ph.D. thesis, University of East Anglia, 1975; Deryck Beyleveld, 'Transcendentalism and Realism', unpublished paper, 1980. Note that this is a different and more precise sense of rationalism than that used in David Sylvan and Barry Glasner, *A Rationalist Methodology for the Social Sciences* (Oxford: Blackwell, 1985). For them, the 'New Social Realism' is a variant of rationalism.
42. Hollis, *Models of Man*, p. 179.
43. Bhaskar, *A Realist Theory of Science*, p. 211.
44. Ibid., p. 174.
45. Immanuel Kant, *The Critique of Pure Reason*, A.369. (Tr. Norman Kemp-Smith (London: Macmillan, 1964), pp. 345 f.)
46. Bhaskar, 'Forms of Realism', *Philosophica*, vol. 15, no. 1, 1975, pp. 100 ff.
47. Beyleveld, 'Epistemological Foundations', p. 22.
48. Bhaskar, *A Realist Theory of Science*, p. 249. Cf. *The Possibility of Naturalism* (Brighton: Harvester, 1979), pp. 73 f.
49. Beyleveld, 'Transcendentalism and Realism', p. 29.
50. Ibid., p. 27.
51. Rorty, *Consequences of Pragmatism*, p. xxvi.
52. A more serious formulation can be found in a recent article by Jonathan Bennett, in P. Bieri *et al.* (eds), *Transcendental Arguments and Science* (Dordrecht: Reidel, 1979), pp. 47 f.
53. Beyleveld, 'Transcendentalism and Realism', p. 41.
54. Bhaskar, *A Realist Theory of Science*, pp. 172 f.
55. Beyleveld, 'Transcendentalism and Realism', p. 42.
56. Hollis, *Models of Man*, p. 171.
57. Putnam, *Meaning and the Moral Sciences*.
58. Bhaskar, *A Realist Theory of Science*, p. 64.
59. Ibid., p. 57.

3 Realism and Social Science

1. Bhaskar, *A Realist Theory of Science*, p. 250.
2. See Outhwaite, *Concept Formation in Social Science*, chapter 5.
3. *A System of Logic*, 7th edn (London: Longmans, 1868), book 6, chapter 7, p. 466. Cf. Steven Lukes, 'Methodological Individualism Reconsidered', *British Journal of Sociology*, vol. 19, 1968. Reprinted in Lukes, *Essays in Social Theory* (London: Macmillan, 1977).
4. Pierre Bourdieu, *Outline of a Theory of Practice* (Cambridge: Cambridge University Press, 1977), p. 203, no. 49. Although Bourdieu repeatedly insists

upon this principle, his metatheory seems in practice closer to the position argued for in this book.

5. Cf. M. von Cranach and R. Harré (eds) *The Analysis of Action* (Cambridge: Cambridge University Press, 1982), p. 31.
6. Hollis, *Models of Man*, p. 21 and *passim*.
7. Bhaskar, *The Possibility of Naturalism*, p. 3.
8. Ibid., p. 31.
9. Trevor Pateman has pointed out that this is a gross over-statement; the wild boy of Aveyron presumably performed intentional acts before he encountered human society. It seems to me however that the statement holds, when qualified along the lines of p. 48 above.
10. Ibid., pp. 43 f.
11. Ibid., p. 51.
12. Cf. in particular the work of Anthony Giddens.
13. Harré, *Social Being*, p. 237. (Cf. p. 349: 'After all, in this work I am trying to locate the social psychological processes and not to solve the great traditional problems of sociology!')
14. Ibid., p. 94.
15. Bhaskar, *The Possibility of Naturalism*, pp. 48 f.
16. Ted Benton, 'Realism and Social Science', *Radical Philosophy*, no. 27, 1981.
17. Bhaskar, *The Possibility of Naturalism*, p. 60.
18. Ibid., p. 59.
19. See Outhwaite, *Concept Formation in Social Science*, pp. 51–67.
20. Of course the natural sciences are subject to periodic revolutions, but there usually emerges fairly rapidly a consensus on a limited number of post-revolutionary research programmes, and in general a cumulative development of knowledge, at least empirical knowledge. (Cf. Hesse, *Revolutions and Reconstructions*, pp. 176 f.).
21. A. Giddens, *New Rules of Sociological Method* (London: Hutchinson, 1976), p. 13.
22. L. Goldmann, *Marxisme et sciences humaines* (Paris: Gallimard, 1970), p. 250.
23. Bhaskar, *The Possibility of Naturalism*, p. 63.
24. W. I. and D. S. Thomas, *The Child in America* (New York: Knopf, 1982), p. 572.
25. Bhaskar, *The Possibility of Naturalism*, pp. 63 ff.
26. Cf. Karl Marx, *Capital*, vol. 1 (Harmondsworth: Penguin, 1976), pp. 173 f.
27. See, for example, Derek Sayer, *Marx's Method. Ideology, Science and Critique in Capital* (Brighton: Harvester Press, 1979), and Bhaskar's entry on 'Realism' in Tom Bottomore (ed.), *A Dictionary of Marxist Thought*, (Oxford: Blackwell, 1983), pp. 407–9.
28. I discuss this further in Chapter 6. See also Gillian Rose, *Hegel Contra Sociology* (London: Athlone, 1981), p. 1. Rose argues that 'The very idea of a scientific sociology, whether Marxist or non-Marxist, is only possible as a form of neo-Kantianism.'
29. Emile Durkheim, Review of A. Labriola, *Essays on the Materialist Conception of History*, in Ken Thompson (ed.), *Readings from Emile Durkheim* (Chichester: Ellis Horwood, 1985), p. 28.
30. Compare, for example, chapter 2 of *The Possibility of Naturalism* with *Social Being*, pp. 19 ff., 139 ff., 237, 348 ff. and 356.
31. Cf. Hollis and Nell, *Rational Economic Man*, chapter 8.
32. 'Theory and Value in the Social Sciences', in C. Hookway and P. Pettit (eds), *Action and Interpretation* (Cambridge: Cambridge University Press, 1978).

Reprinted in Mary Hesse, *Revolutions and Reconstructions in the Philosophy of Science* (Brighton: Harvester, 1980).
33. Bhaskar, *The Possibility of Naturalism*, p. 59.

4 Realism and Hermeneutics

1. Jürgen Habermas, *Zur Logik der Sozialwissenschaften*, 2nd edn (Frankfurt: Suhrkamp, 1971), p. 72.
2. John B. Thompson, *Critical Hermeneutics* (Cambridge: Cambridge University Press, 1981).
3. Hans-Georg Gadamer, *Truth and Method* (London: Sheed & Ward, 1975). Some passages in this chapter have already been published in my contribution to Quentin Skinner (ed.), *The Return of Grand Theory in the Human Sciences* (Cambridge: Cambridge University Press, 1985).
4. 'Rhetorik, Hermeneutik und Ideologiekritik', in *Hermeneutik und Ideologiekritik* (Frankfurt: Suhrkamp, 1971), p. 64. Translated in 'The Scope and Function of Hermeneutical Reflection' in H.-G. Gadamer, *Philosophical Hermeneutics* (Berkeley: University of California Press, 1976), p. 25. Cf. the slogan in *Truth and Method*, p. 432: 'Being that can be understood is language'.
5. Cf. Gadamer's recent collection of articles: *Reason in the Age of Science* (Cambridge, Mass.: MIT Press, 1982).
6. Gadamer, *Philosophical Hermeneutics*, p. 3.
7. Gadamer, *Truth and Method*, p. 412.
8. Gadamer, *Philosophical Hermeneutics*, p. 39.
9. Cf. for example, E. J. Dijksterhuis, *The Mechanisation of the World-Picture* (Oxford: Oxford University Press, 1961).
10. Gadamer, *Truth and Method*, pp. 5 ff.
11. Gadamer, *Philosophical Hermeneutics*, p. 40.
12. The essay from which I have been quoting is a response to Habermas's 1967 critique in his *Zur Logik der Sozialwissenschaften*. Habermas continued the exchange in his contribution to Gadamer's festschrift, *Hermeneutik und Dialektik I* (Tübingen: Mohr, 1970). This essay, entitled 'The hermeneutic claim to universality', is translated in Josef Bleicher (ed.), *Contemporary Hermeneutics* (London: Routledge & Kegan Paul, 1970). See also Gadamer's reply in *Hermeneutik und Ideologiekritik*.
13. Gadamer, *Hermeneutik und Ideologiekritik*, pp. 66 f.; *Philosophical Hermeneutics*, p. 27. This is an extremely obscure passage and the translation, which Gadamer is said to have corrected (p. vii), diverges a good deal from the original.
14. Gadamer, *Truth and Method*, p. xiii.
15. Cf. my article on Gadamer in *The Return of Grand Theory*.
16. For an overview, see Bleicher (ed.), *Contemporary Hermeneutics*, and Bleicher, *The Hermeneutic Imagination* (London: Routledge & Kegan Paul, 1982).
17. Gadamer, *Truth and Method*, p. 253.
18. Anthony Giddens, *Central Problems in Social Theory* (London: Macmillan, 1979), p. 248.
19. Giddens, *New Rules of Sociological Method* (London: Hutchinson, 1976), p. 13.
20. Max Weber, *Roscher and Knies* (New York: Free Press, 1975) pp. 217 f.
21. Giddens, *New Rules of Sociological Method*, p. 158.
22. Alfred Schutz, *The Phenomenology of the Social World* (London: Heinemann, 1972), p. 10.

23. Josef Bleicher, *The Hermeneutic Imagination*, pp. 106–14.
24. Alfred Schutz, 'Choice and the Social Sciences', in L. Embree (ed.), *Life World and Consciousness. Essays in Memory of Aaron Gurwitsch* (Evanston, Ill.: Northwestern University Press, 1972), p. 583.
25. Richard Grathoff, *The Theory of Social Action*.
26. One of several formulations of this principle is the following in Alfred Schutz, *Collected Papers vol. I. The Problem of Social Reality* (The Hague: Nijhoff, 1962), pp. 34 f. 'Each term in a scientific model of human action must be constructed in such a way that a human act performed within the life-world by an individual actor in the way indicated by the typical construct would be understandable for the actor himself as well as for his fellow-men in terms of common-sense interpretations of everyday life.'
27. Schutz, 'Choice and the Social Sciences', p. 582.
28. Cf. Bleicher, *The Hermeneutic Imagination*, pp. 133 ff.
29. J. Habermas, *Theorie des Kommunikativen Handelns*, vol. 2 (Frankfurt: Suhrkamp, 1981), p. 212.
30. P. Berger and T. Luckmann, *The Social Construction of Reality* (Harmondsworth: Penguin, 1967).
31. Habermas, *Zur Logik der Sozialwissenschaften*, pp. 243 f.
32. Giddens, *New Rules of Sociological Method*, pp. 158 f.
33. Giddens, *Central Problems in Social Theory* (London: Macmillan, 1979), p. 5. Trevor Pateman has pointed out that the term '*stock*' of knowledge' is misleading, since such knowledge must also include ways of operating with that knowledge (inference mechanisms, etc.). Cf. Stephen P. Stich, 'Beliefs and Subdoxastic States', *Philosophy of Science*, vol. 45, 1978, pp. 499–518.
34. Ibid., pp. 5 f.
35. Paul Ricoeur, *Freud and Philosophy. An Essay on Interpretation* (New Haven: Yale University Press, 1970), p. 26. The latter approach, Ricoeur argues, is dominated by Marx, Nietzsche and Freud.
36. Gadamer, *Philosophical Hermeneutics*, p. 26.
37. Ibid., p. 33.
38. Ibid., p. 42.
39. 'Hermeneutics and the Critique of Ideology' in Paul Ricoeur, *Hermeneutics and the Human Sciences*, edited and translated by John B. Thompson (Cambridge: Cambridge University Press; Paris: Editions de la Maison des Sciences de l'Homme, 1981).
40. Habermas, 'The Hermeneutic Claim to Universality', in Bleicher, *Contemporary Hermeneutics*, p. 190.
41. Ibid., pp. 186 f.
42. Habermas, *Zur Logik der Sozialwissenschaften*, p. 289.
43. Ibid., p. 287.
44. Gadamer, *Philosophical Hermeneutics*, pp. 31 f.
45. Habermas, *Zur Logik der Sozialwissenschaften*, pp. 290–304.
46. Habermas, 'The Hermeneutic Claim to Universality', p. 189.
47. Habermas, *Zur Logik der Sozialwissenschaften*, p. 304.
48. Habermas, 'The Hermeneutic Claim to Universality', p. 208.
49. Ibid., p. 203.
50. Cf. Bleicher, *The Hermeneutic Imagination*, Conclusion.

5 Realism and Critical Theory

1. See in particular David Held, *Introduction to Critical Theory* (London: Hutchinson, 1980).
2. Max Horkheimer, 'Traditional and Critical Theory' (1937), reprinted in Paul Connerton (ed.) *Critical Sociology* (Harmondsworth: Penguin, 1976), pp. 224 f.
3. Max Horkheimer, 'Zum Rationalismusstreit in der gegenwärtigen Philosophie' (1934), reprinted in Max Horkheimer, *Kritische Theorie*, vol. 1 (Frankfurt: Suhrkamp, 1968), p. 146.
4. Max Horkheimer and Theodor W. Adorno, *Dialectic of Enlightenment* (1944). English translation (London: Allen Lane, 1972), p. xi.
5. Habermas, *The Theory of Communicative Action*, vol. 1 (London: Heinemann, 1984), p. 386. Cf. Helmut Dubiel, *Wissenschaftsorganisation und politische Erfahrung* (Frankfurt: Suhrkamp, 1978).
6. T. Adorno *et al.*, *The Positivist Dispute in German Sociology* (London: Heinemann, 1976).
7. Habermas, *Knowledge and Human Interests* (London: Heinemann, 1972), p. vii. Cf. also his 'literature report', *Zur Logik der Sozialwissenschaften*, originally published in 1967. *Theorie des Kommunikativen Handelns* takes a similar form.
8. Habermas, *Strukturwandel der Öffentlichkeit* (Neuwied: Luchterhand, 1962), pp. 278 ff. This book is still not available in English, though there is a French translation (*L'Espace publique*, Paris: Payot, 1978).
9. This is published as an appendix to the English translation.
10. Habermas, *Knowledge and Human Interests*, p. vii.
11. Ibid., pp. 68 f.
12. Ibid., p. vii.
13. Norman Stockman, *Anti-Positivist Theories of the Sciences* (Dordrecht: Riedel, 1983), p. 101.
14. Ibid., p. 107.
15. Jürgen Habermas, 'A Postscript to *Knowledge and Human Interests*', *Philosophy of the Social Sciences*, vol. 3, no. 2, 1973, p. 180.
16. *Theorie des Kommunikativen Handelns*, vol 2 (Frankfurt: Suhrkamp, 1981), p. 586.
17. 'A Reply to My Critics', in John B. Thompson and David Held (eds), *Habermas. Critical Debates* (London: Macmillan, 1982), p. 233.
18. Habermas, *Knowledge and Human Interests*, pp. 68 f.
19. Ibid., Appendix, pp. 309 f.
20. Ibid., p. 191.
21. The interest in communication which governs the hermeneutic sciences plays a somewhat different role, since here the object domain is already constituted by the framework of ordinary language. (Cf. ibid., pp. 191 ff.)
22. Ibid., p. 194.
23. Cf. Mary Hesse, *Revolutions and Reconstructions in the Philosophy of Science*, especially pp. 182–6.
24. Habermas, *Knowledge and Human Interests*, chapter 5. He also, of course, adopts a basically Peircean 'consensus theory of truth'.
25. Thomas McCarthy, *The Critical Theory of Jürgen Habermas*, 2nd edn (Cambridge: Polity, 1984), p. 65.
26. Bhaskar, *A Realist Theory of Science*, p. 249.
27. McCarthy, *The Critical Theory of Jürgen Habermas*, pp. 110 f.
28. Ibid., p. 124.

29. 'Postscript', *Philosophy of the Social Sciences*, vol. 3, no. 2, 1973.
30. Habermas, *Theory and Practice* (London: Heinemann, 1974), pp. 19 f. Cf. the postscript to *Knowledge and Human Interests*, pp. 166 and 168–74.
31. J. Habermas and N. Luhmann, *Theorie der Gesellschaft oder Sozialtechnologie – Was Leistet die Systemforschung?* (Frankfurt: Suhrkamp, 1971), p. 206.
32. Ibid., p. 212.
33. Ibid., p. 214.
34. McCarthy, *The Critical Theory of Jürgen Habermas*, pp. 278 f.
35. Habermas, *Knowledge and Human Interests*, Appendix, p. 310.
36. 'Postscript', p. 182.
37. Cf. Habermas, 'Towards a Theory of Communicative Competence', *Inquiry*, vol. 13, 1970.
38. Habermas, *Communication and the Evolution of Society* (Boston: Beacon Press, 1979), p. 16.
39. Ibid., cf. the passage in his Christian Gauss lectures at Princeton in 1970–71 reprinted in *Vorstudien und Ergänzungen zur Theorie des Kommunikativen Handelns* (Frankfurt: Suhrkamp, 1984), pp. 18 f.
40. W. V. O. Quine, 'Methodological Reflections on Current Linguistic Theory', in D. Davidson and G. Harman (eds), *Semantics of Natural Language* (Dordrecht: Reidel, 1972), pp. 442 f.
41. Habermas, *Theorie des Kommunikativen Handelns*, vol. 2, p. 179.
42. Ibid., p. 223.
43. Ibid., p. 224.
44. Ibid., p. 227.
45. The form of *Theory of Communicative Action* is very like Parsons's *Structure of Social Action*; the aim is to demonstrate a convergence of central themes of classical sociological theories towards Habermas's own emergent conception. Cf. vol. 1, preface, p. 7.
46. Stockman, *Anti-Positivist Theories of the Sciences*, p. 256.
47. Ibid., p. 207.
48. Ibid., p. 217. The quotation is from Habermas, *Theory and Practice* (London: Heinemann, 1974), p. 210.
49. Habermas, *The Theory of Communicative Action*, p. 337.
50. Habermas, 'Erläuterungen zum Begriff der kommunikativen Handelns', reported in *Vorstudien*, p. 606.
51. Habermas, 'Wahrheitstheorien', *Vorstudien*, p. 133.
52. Bhaskar, 'Emergence, Explanation and Emancipation', in Paul Secord (ed.), *Explaining Human Behaviour* (Beverly Hills: Sage, 1982); 'Scientific Explanation and Human Emancipation', *Radical Philosophy* 26, 1980. Cf. Roy Edgley, 'Marx's Revolutionary Science', in J. Mepham and D. H. Ruben (eds), *Issues in Marxist Philosophy*, vol. III (Brighton: Harvester, 1979).
53. Stockman, *Anti-Positivist Theories of the Sciences*, p. 229.
54. See Habermas's *Legitimation Crisis* (Boston: Beacon Press, 1975).

6 Critical Hermeneutics, Realism and the Sociological Tradition

1. Karl Marx, *Grundrisse* (Harmondsworth: Penguin, 1973), pp. 106, 331.
2. Marx, *Capital*, vol. 1 (Harmondsworth: Penguin, 1976), p. 174.
3. Derek Sayer, *Marx's Method* 2nd edn (Brighton: Harvester, 1979), pp. 8 ff.
4. *Capital*, vol. 1, p. 127.
5. I. I. Rubin, *Essays on Marx's Theory of Value* (Montreal: Black Rose Books, 1973). First published in 1928.

6. See also J. Mepham and D.-H. Ruben (eds) *Issues in Marxist Philosophy*, vols 1–3, (Brighton: Harvester, 1979).

7. See, for example, Leszek Kolakowski, 'Karl Marx and the Classical Definition of Truth', in Kolakowski, *Marxism and Beyond* (London: Pall Mall Press, 1969; Paladin, 1971); Alfred Schmidt, *The Concept of Nature in Marx* (London: New Left Books, 1971); Nathan Rotenstreich, *Basic Problems of Marx's Philosophy* (New York, Bobbs-Merrill, 1965).

8. Georg Lukács, *History and Class Consciousness* (London: Merlin, 1971), p. 130.

9. Cf. Outhwaite, *Concept Formation*, pp. 85 f., 143 ff.

10. See Chapter 7 below.

11. On the other hand, Marx's lack of precision in the area of metatheory has generated a good deal of unnecessary confusion.

12. Cf. Douglas House, 'Durkheim and the Realist Philosophy of Social Science', *Sociological Analysis and Theory*, vol. 5, no. 2, 1975, pp. 237–51.

13. Emile Durkheim, *The Rules of Sociological Method* (London: Routledge & Kegan Paul, 1952) ch. 5.

14. Emile Durkheim, *The Elementary Forms of the Religious Life* (London: Allen & Unwin, 1915).

15. Gillian Rose, *Hegel Contra Sociology*, p. 1.

16. Cf. Russell Keat and John Urry, *Social Theory as Science*, 2nd edn (London: Routledge & Kegan Paul, 1975, 1982), pp. 84 f.; Ted Benton, *The Philosophical Foundations of the Three Sociologies* (London: Routledge & Kegan Paul, 1977), p. 100.

17. Durkheim, *Rules of Sociological Method*, pp. 34 ff.

18. Keat and Urry, *Social Theory as Science*, p. 85.

19. Max Weber, *Economy and Society*, vol. 1 (New York: Bedminster Press, 1968), p. 19 (translation modified). He first uses the term 'Wirklichkeitswissenschaft' in *Roscher and Knies* (New York: Free Press, 1975), p. 55, though not yet in relation to sociology. Cf. Horst Baier, *Von der Erkenntnistheorie zur Wirklichkeitswissenschaft* (Habilitationsschrift: University of Münster, 1969), p. 141.

20. 'Objectivity in Social Science & Social Policy' in Max Weber, *The Methodology of the Social Sciences* (New York: Free Press, 1949), p. 106.

21. Ibid., p. 94.

22. Ibid., p. 106.

23. Ibid., p. 94.

24. *Economy and Society*, vol. I, p. 4.

25. Cf. Baier, *Von der Erkenntnistheorie* . . ., pp. 194–202. See also, in particular, H. Rickert, *Die Grenzen der naturwissenschaftlichen Begriffsbildung* (Tübingen: J. C. B. Mohr, 1902); Carl Menger, *Problems of Economics and Sociology* (Urbana: University of Illinois Press, 1963).

26. Quoted in Marianne Weber, *Max Weber: A Biography* (New York: Wiley, 1975), p. 677.

27. Weber, 'Objectivity', p. 72. I have used the much better translation provided by Thomas Burger, *Max Weber's Theory of Concept Formation* (Durham, NC: Duke University Press, 1976).

28. 'The Logic of the Cultural Sciences', in Max Weber's, *The Methodology of the Social Sciences*, pp. 185 f. Translation modified.

29. Weber, *Roscher and Knies*, p. 190.

30. Weber, 'Objectivity', p. 112.

31. Ibid., p. 106.

32. Ibid., pp. 83 f.

33. Cf. Harold Bershady, *Ideology and Social Knowledge* (Oxford: Blackwell, 1973).
34. Talcott Parsons, *The Structure of Social Action* (New York: Free Press, paperback edn, 1968, pp. 101 ff.).
35. Ibid., p. 730.
36. Cf. Thomas Burger, 'Talcott Parsons, the Problem of Order in Sociology and the Program of an Analytical Sociology', *American Journal of Sociology*, vol. 83, no. 2, p. 324.
37. Ibid., pp. 330 f.
38. Ibid., p. 330.
39. Ibid., p. 332.
40. It is interesting to note that Althusser makes a similar claim about the relationship between sciences and their objects, and I think it could be argued that it has similarly unfortunate consequences for his very different substantive theorising about social reality.
41. Note that this principle has not always been adequately applied in realist theories. Rom Harré operates with a rather curious distinction between the domains of sociology and social psychology *Social Being*, p. 349, which Bhaskar has at times taken up (*The Possibility of Naturalism*, p. 45).

7 Conclusion: Action, Structure and Realist Philosophy

1. Rom Harré and P. F. Secord, *The Explanation of Social Behaviour* (Oxford: Blackwell, 1972), ch. 5.
2. Lukes, 'Methodological Individualism Reconsidered', in D. Emmet and A. MacIntyre (eds) *Sociological Theory and Philosophical Analysis* (London: Macmillan, 1970), p. 77.
3. Outhwaite, *Concept Formation*, ch. 5.
4. Bhaskar, *Naturalism*, p. 43.
5. J.-P. Sartre, *Critique of Dialectical Reason* (London: New Left Books, 1976); Alain Touraine, *Sociologie de l'Action* (Paris: Seuil, 1965).
6. Cf. Scott Lash and John Urry, 'The New Marxism of Collective Action: A Critical Analysis', *Sociology*, vol. 18, no. 1, 1984, pp. 33–50.
7. 'Theories of Social Action', in Tom Bottomore and Robert Nisbet (eds), *A History of Sociological Analysis* (London: Heinemann, 1978), p. 367.
8. Giddens, *New Rules of Sociological Method*, p. 161.
9. Giddens, *Profiles and Critiques in Social Theory* (London: Macmillan, 1982), p. 38.
10. One should note however that, like most social theory, it skates around issues to do with the intrinsic or pre-social powers of human beings – issues which are crucial to psychology and linguistics. See Trevor Pateman, *Language in Mind and Language in Society* (Oxford: Clarendon Press, 1987).
11. John Urry, *The Anatomy of Capitalist Societies* (London: Macmillan, 1981); Keat and Urry, *Social Theory as Science*; Urry, 'Science, Realism and the Social', *Philosophy of Social Science*, vol. 12, 1982, pp. 311–18.
12. Urry, *The Anatomy of Capitalist Societies*, p. 8.
13. For a Marxist account which tries to deal with these problems, see Karl Liebknecht, *Studien über die Bewegungsgesetze der gesellschaftlichen Entwicklung* (1922, new edition edited by O. K. Flechtheim, Hamburg, 1974).
14. Urry, *The Anatomy of Capitalist Societies*.
15. Ian Hacking, *Representing and Intervening* (Cambridge: Cambridge University Press, 1983), p. 23.

16. Rom Harré, 'Images of Society and Social Icons'.
17. Ibid.
18. Bhaskar, *The Possibility of Naturalism*, pp. 48 f.
19. Giddens, *New Rules*, p. 13.
20. Bourdieu, *Outline of a Theory of Practice*, p. 203.
21. Martin Albrow, 'The Concept of "the Social" in the Work of Marx and Weber', unpublished paper from conference on 'Karl Marx and Max Weber', Duisburg, 1981).
22. P. F. Strawson, *Individuals* (London: Methuen, 1959).
23. Susan James, *The Content of Social Explanation* (Cambridge: Cambridge University Press, 1985), pp. 6 f.
24. Barry Hindess, 'Actors and Social Relations', in Mark Wardell and Stephen Turner (eds), *Sociological Theory in Transition* (Boston: Allen & Unwin, 1986), p. 119.
25. Cf. ibid., p. 117.
26. Hollis and Nell, *Rational Economic Man*; Mary Farmer, 'Rational Action in Economic and Social Theory: Some Misunderstandings', *Archives Européennes de Sociologie*, vol. 23, 1982, pp. 179–97.
27. See, for example, T. M. Bloomfield, 'Psychoanalysis: a Human Science?', *Journal for the Theory of Social Behaviour*, vol. 9, no. 3, 1979, pp. 271–87; David Will, 'Psychoanalysis as a Human Science', *British Journal of Medical Psychology*, vol. 53, no. 3, 1980, pp. 201–11.
28. For an overview, see Trevor Pateman, 'Philosophy of Linguistics', in Richard Coates *et al.* (eds), *New Horizons in Linguistics 2* (Harmondsworth: Penguin, forthcoming).
29. Social scientists, for example, now have an excellent and very accessible methodological text written from a realist standpoint: Andrew Sayer, *Method in Social Science* (London: Hutchinson, 1984).
30. Cf. Norman Stockman, *Anti-Positivist Theories of the Sciences*.

Further Reading

Realism

Benton, Ted, *The Philosophical Foundations of the Three Sociologies* (London: Routledge & Kegan Paul, 1977).
——, 'Realism and Social Science', *Radical Philosophy*, no. 27, 1981.
Bhaskar, Roy, *A Realist Theory of Science*, 2nd edn (Brighton: Harvester, 1978).
——, *The Possibility of Naturalism* (Brighton: Harvester, 1979).
——, *Scientific Realism and Human Emancipation* (London: Verso, 1986).
Harré, Rom, *Varieties of Realism* (Oxford: Blackwell, 1986).
Keat, Russell and Urry, John, *Social Theory as Science*, 2nd edn (London: Routledge & Kegan Paul, 1982).
Outhwaite, William, *Concept Formation in Social Science* (London: Routledge & Kegan Paul, 1983).
——, 'Laws and Explanations in Sociology', in John Hughes *et al.* (eds), *Classic Disputes in Sociology* (London: George Allen & Unwin, 1987).
Sayer, Andrew, *Method in Social Science* (London: Hutchinson, 1984).

Hermeneutics and critical theory

Bauman, Zygmunt, *Hermeneutics and Social Science* (London: Hutchinson, 1978).
Bleicher, Josef, *Contemporary Hermeneutics* (London: Routledge & Kegan Paul, 1980).
——, *The Hermeneutic Imagination* (London: Routledge & Kegan Paul, 1982).
Dallmayr, Fred and McCarthy, Thomas, *Understanding and Social Inquiry* (Indianapolis: Notre Dame University Press, 1977).
Held, David, *Introduction to Critical Theory* (London: Hutchinson, 1980).
Held, David and Thompson, John (eds), *Habermas. Critical Debates* (London: Macmillan, 1982).
McCarthy, Thomas, *The Critical Theory of Jürgen Habermas*, 2nd edn (Cambridge: Polity, 1984).
Outhwaite, William, *Understanding Social Life*, 2nd edn (Lewes: Jean Stroud, 1986).
Roderick, Rick, *Habermas and the Foundations of Critical Theory* (London: Macmillan, 1986).
Thompson, John, *Critical Hermeneutics. A Study in the Thought of Paul Ricoeur and Jürgen Habermas* (Cambridge: Cambridge University Press, 1981).

Index

133